BEAT

PARKY

A Journey To Let Parkinson's Disease
Define My Family's Legacy... For The
Better.

Michael Cheung

First paperback edition May 2020

ISBN 9798642545928 (Paperback)

To my parents, Man Ki Joseph Cheung and Kit Ling Kitty Tse, and the love of my life, Chelsey Ann Bogaczewicz.

You guys make my heart so full.

How do you find meaning in a riddle with no answer?

Table of Contents

Foreword:

Growing up in a Chinese immigrant household, it was customary to be reluctant to inconvenience others and to avoid uncomfortable conversations. Maybe this was why I never approached Mike on the subject of his father when we were younger.

Mike and I have always been close growing up. Our families immigrated to Canada together and we did not know many people here when we first arrived. He and I spent endless hours together during our childhood and adolescence filled mostly with sports, video games, family gatherings, and the occasional family vacation. We consider each other brothers instead of cousins. And in some ways, his parents, who are my aunt and uncle, influenced me just as much as my own parents during my childhood.

Despite all our time together throughout the years, the subject of my uncle being diagnosed with Parkinson's rarely came up in discussion. I can't quite remember when I first started noticing my uncle's shaking, but I do remember hesitating to ask on numerous occasions. Part of me didn't want to be rude, but the other part was afraid of hearing the truth. As the signs and symptoms became more apparent, nobody openly acknowledged it. Our families carried on dinners and gatherings like normal in the proceeding years. This became how things werc for some time. There was an unspoken understanding between us that my uncle's health was declining and everyone would do their best to make things seem as normal as possible.

I can't remember when the exact conversation took place, but eventually my mom told me my uncle had Parkinson's. As she did her best to hold back tears, I felt reluctant to ask her further questions and inconvenience her into explaining why something so unfair had happened to her brother and Mike's family. How can you explain something like this to a fifteen year old? I also remember after the sadness momentarily dissipated, Mike was the first person I thought of. I couldn't even imagine how he felt and how hard it must have been to keep it to himself all these years. Even though I had all these questions, I never ended up asking him directly until we were much older, probably for reasons similar to why I never asked my mom.

Reading Beat Parky reminded me in many ways of the moment my mom told me about my uncle. Hearing Mike's perspective on the situation and reliving moments of our childhood in a different light was heartbreaking, but also relieving. It answered many of the questions I had growing up. It also opened up the possibility for further conversations with my cousin on a subject our families were too reluctant to talk about openly. This is an opportunity I won't put to waste.

This story has also reminded me that inspiration is anywhere if you just look for it. Beat Parky helped me realize how much of an impact Mike and his dad have had in my life.

My uncle inspired me to find appreciation in the everyday. Watching him go through his journey of fighting Parkinson's and overcoming setback after setback without ever complaining about the pain or how hard it is has made me reflect on how grateful I am for simple things I take for granted, such as being able to walk, wake up pain free every morning, and continue to stay active through sports. His mental toughness is second to none and this is something I try to replicate in my approach to every challenge I face.

Lastly, through this book, Mike has inspired me to challenge the Asian cultural norms we grew up with and gain the courage to approach uncomfortable subjects with people I care about. Observing his transformation through this journey showed me how a shift in mindset is the key. This will be something I will work towards the rest of my life. You can't always control what happens to you, but you can control how you react to the situation. Mike has taught me to embrace my struggles and make them a facet of my identity. Only then will I become resilient and mentally strong enough to be successful.

John F. Kennedy once said, "As we express our gratitude, we must never forget that the highest appreciation is not to utter words, but to live by them." This is the way I choose to honor Mike and his father's legacy.

- Wilfrid Lok

(Photo Cred: Kushal Pachchigar)

Wilfrid and Michael at the first #BeerParky fundraiser

Introduction:

One of humanity's greatest mysteries is the meaning of life, and almost everybody you ask will have a different answer. Is it to live a happy and fruitful life with loved ones? Perhaps it is to make as much money as possible and spend it however your heart desires? Or maybe it is to leave the world a better place for future generations to experience?

Regardless of what you think it may be, we all strive to live long, happy, meaningful, and successful lives. Sadly, this isn't possible for a significant portion of the human population.

How people end up with subpar lives happens in a multitude of ways, with examples including:

- Being born with a disease/illness
- Getting into a car accident
- Surrounding yourself with the wrong people
- Committing a crime
- Loved ones dying in an accident
- Forming an addiction to drugs and alcohol
- Falling victim to a crime
- Making unhealthy lifestyle choices

As you can see from the list above, there are a number of ways people end up with substandard lives; some you earn, and others you don't deserve. The worst part is not only will these negatively affect your life if they happen to you, but they will also have a personal impact if they occur to anyone close to you, especially family members.

One of the more significant misfortunes that touches a large portion of humanity is terminal or life-altering health problems. This can be anything from cancer, blindness, dementia, obesity, multiple sclerosis, allergies, autism, diabetes and more.

The list is depressingly long, frustratingly common, and tends to negatively affect how we live our lives.

I know what you are thinking, individuals who have mental or physical disabilities can still live a fulfilling life. I'm not saying that if any of the aforementioned maladies happen to you or a loved one then you are 100% sure to have a below average life, especially if it occurs at a later stage in life or your symptoms aren't as severe. There are many people who have persevered through extenuating circumstances to achieve unthinkable success. They even often become famous because of their stories and everything they have overcome. Think Stephen Hawking, Michael J Fox, Ray Charles, Helen Keller, Franklin D Roosevelt, Claude Monet, Stevie Wonder, etc.

Unfortunately, this is not a common outcome.

The majority of us suffer or knows a loved one who

suffers from a life-altering disease or terminal diagnosis. Not only are we forced to deal with the consequences and adapt to a new "normal", but so do our family and friends.

When faced with this, we often resort to one of these common responses:

1. There are people dying in third world countries due to starvation and other preventable causes who would gladly trade places with me. It can always be worse.
2. No one cares or wants to hear about my problems; I should keep them to myself.
3. Why do all of these horrible things happen to me? Life is not fair.
4. Maybe there was something I could have done to prevent this from happening?

Life is short and we only live once, so our goal should be to make the most out of it regardless of our circumstances. In the end, what choice do we really have? Yet, none of these responses make us feel better about the situation or turn it into a positive.

Most of the time, they lead us to hide our emotions until we eventually spiral out of control, to the point where we either resort to drugs, alcohol, and other vices, or use it as an excuse to explain why our lives didn't turn out the way we wanted it to. After all, life can really suck due to circumstances outside of your own control.

Trust me, I've been there… and denied it for many years as you'll see.

However, I am of the opinion that life is not about what happens to you, but rather how you react to it. You are only a victim if you allow yourself to be.

If none of the generic mindsets listed above work, how should we be tackling these unfortunate situations to mitigate their effects? How are we supposed to find happiness and meaning in the face of unspeakably depressing circumstances? How do we succeed in the giant mind game known as life?

If you have a loved one who currently suffers from a life changing disease/illness/health condition, I believe you will gain lots of value from this book, especially if you are like me and feel frustratingly useless while watching a cherished family member suffer. Life may not currently be great for someone we care about who is affected by illness - that is the harsh reality sometimes, but we can certainly strive towards making things better for them.

The daily goal for every individual is to be better than our present circumstances, regardless of whether misfortune plays a part in the story.

Those of you reading this from the perspective of someone who currently has a life-altering disease/illness, I hope you know that your bravery, strength, resilience, and courage is inspiring others to be better and live life to the fullest, even if they may not express it to you directly.

Keep fighting.

If you are lucky enough to not be in either of these positions, there are still lots of lessons and strategies in this book that can be applied to everyday life or to help a friend who is suffering. We can all stand to learn from those who are less fortunate and be more appreciative of our blessings. Doing so will only improve the quality of our lives.

I'm not saying I have all of the answers, nor am I an expert in psychology or human biology. In fact, I can't even tell you that what has worked for me so far will help you. After all, every situation is different. All I know is that through the development of the upcoming seven concepts in this book, I was able to turn an extremely unfortunate break for my father into my greatest blessing, and I want to help you do the same.

Not that I'd ever hope that this would happen to my family if I could go back in time and rewrite the future, but I certainly wouldn't pass up the advantage of having to live through this. The disease isn't a gift or blessing, but the response has been.

Thankfully, that is 100% in our control.

I guarantee these concepts will be present in every story, and perhaps even more vibrant and visible than in mine. There is nothing extraordinary about me, and I know a lot of you reading are capable of doing far better than I have so far turning misfortune into blessing.

I am sharing my family's story in the hopes that this will help give you the tools to make the best of your situation and become happier, which will ultimately become my father's legacy. While I'm fortunate to still have my dad with me, circumstances outside of his control have limited the time and ability that he has left to finish molding his legacy himself.

But the thing about legacies is that they are immortal, and don't end after the person has passed away. Unfortunate events don't just affect a single individual, and every person touched has the ability to write their own storybook ending in that person's honour. After all, how many people can say they helped positively influence another individual's life, let alone what I hope to be the thousands who read this book?

My heart will be so full if that is the legacy that my father leaves behind. Fortunately, I have the capacity to try and make that a reality.

The ending is only sad if you allow it to be.

I'm excited to explore and relive all the past memories and moments that this book will take me through, many suppressed and forgotten because they have been too difficult to address until now.

In a way, this is my greatest form of therapy, so thank you in advance for reading.

My name is Michael Cheung. My father, Man Ki Joseph Cheung, was diagnosed with Early Onset Parkinson's Disease at the age of 45 when I was 12 years old and has had the disease for over 17 years and counting. My mother, Kit Ling Kitty Tse, has been by his side through it all. They are the two strongest people I will ever know.

I am on a mission to let Parkinson's define my family's legacy... for the better.

And this is our story.

Chapter 1: What is Parkinson's?

First off, you may be wondering… what is Parkinson's disease (PD)? Ever since I started sharing my story, I've noticed that the majority of people have heard of Parkinson's, but are not exactly sure what the disease is and how it affects the average person. Oftentimes, researching a disease will lead to finding confusing articles with numerous scientific words that leave you wondering if it is even written in English. Trust me, I know from personal experience when my dad was initially diagnosed. Simply put, people know Parkinson's as the disease Muhammed Ali had when he was still alive and that Michael J. Fox currently suffers from. As a result, I'm going to use this chapter to explain it in the most layman terms possible.

Parkinson's disease is a degenerative brain disorder named after James Parkinson, who published the first description of the disease in 1817, and is currently the fastest growing neurological disorder in the world, even outpacing Alzheimer's disease.[1] It results in the loss of cells in the substantia nigra part of the brain. These cells help to create dopamine, which is a neurotransmitter responsible for sending signals throughout your brain and body to help with movement and cognitive functions.

The list of famous people who have been or are currently affected by Parkinson's disease includes: Reverend Jesse Jackson, Sir Roger Bannister, Muhammed Ali, Michael J Fox, Kirk Gibson, Brian Grant, Neil Diamond, Pope John Paul II, George H.W. Bush, Ozzy Osbourne, Robin Williams, and many, many, more.

The exact causes of the disease are still currently unknown but it is assumed to be a mixture of genetic and environmental factors. The most significant environmental influences include pesticides, solvents, air pollution, and industrial products. Harmful toxins such as paraquat (often found in pesticides to kill weeds) and trichloroethylene (used in solvents for degreasing metal products) are the two most common examples. In addition, avoiding head injuries and trauma, eating healthier, exercise, and consuming caffeine all play a part in decreasing risk of developing Parkinson's. While genetics can also play a part in the chances of obtaining the disease, there are far more cases linked to environmental factors than family history.

The effects of Parkinson's are unique to each individual person, as the symptoms and rate of progression vary case by case. It is often noted that every person diagnosed has a different Parkinson's experience. The main attributes of Parkinson's include but are not limited to the following:

- Slowness of movement/decrease in motor skills
- Trouble sleeping
- Hallucinations during sleep
- Resting tremor
- Postural instability (balance issues)
- Difficulty using the washroom/constipation
- Slurring of speech
- Swallowing issues
- Loss of sense of smell and taste
- Cognitive impairment/dementia
- Difficulties with balance and walking
- Mood disorder/depression
- Muscle pain/stiffness
- Reduced facial expressions/lack of emotion

As you can see from the list above, a Parkinson's diagnosis will be daunting but it is not fatal. In total, there are about 40 symptoms[1], each of which start as mild when initially diagnosed and become more intense over time. You can eventually die from complications, such as trouble swallowing, breathing, or falling due to a lack of motor skills and hitting your head.

While many symptoms are of a physical nature, they are not as obvious as a broken bone, which leads to tremendous difficulty in identifying and diagnosing. A lot of indicators are often diagnosed through observations and can be confused with other diseases or signs of aging. As a result, there is currently no objective test or examination for definitive diagnosis. Combine this with a very limited number of specialists trained in the field of PD and outdated detection tests/techniques, and you can see why many people are misdiagnosed. It is extremely common to hear stories from people who have suspected themselves to have PD but were not diagnosed until years later.

Therefore, there is no exact data documenting people affected by Parkinson's. At the time of this book's initial publishing in mid-2020, it is estimated that there are roughly ten million people worldwide with PD.[2] From those, roughly 10-20% will be diagnosed before the age of 50.[3] My father was one of those people.

Keeping in mind that there is no consistently uniform case of Parkinson's, a day in the life of a person with PD can look like the following:

6:00am: Wake up due to trouble sleeping, aching muscles, and the need to start taking medication in order to be able to move over the course of the day. Since no medication was taken throughout the night, the full effect of Parkinson's is evident. The body is stiff and rigid, and even just getting out of bed is extremely difficult.

6:00am - 7:00am: Bathroom activities to start the day. These will take much longer than usual due to PD symptoms like constipation, trouble urinating, tremors while attempting to brush teeth, and stiffness during showering before medication kicks in. Issues such as hygiene are significant as it is difficult to maintain cleanliness. The average male affected by Parkinson's will need to sit when peeing as a result of a lack of leg strength in standing or the inability to stand still. In addition, it will take people with Parkinson's longer to be able to muster the ability to push bodily fluids and stool out of their system.

7:00am - 7:30am: Breakfast (and eating of any kind) can be frustrating as dyskinesia and tremors make using utensils and moving food from the plate to the mouth difficult. Oftentimes, it takes longer than usual to eat and will result in a messy table top and stained clothes. In addition, issues while swallowing arise and add to the difficulty. Individuals with severely advanced Parkinson's will often be fed through a feeding tube in the hospital.

7:30am - 8:15am: Dressing for the day presents the same challenges as brushing teeth and showering, as tremors and stiffness also make things such as putting on socks and buttoning up shirts extremely difficult. In addition, it can be tricky to balance long enough to be able to put pants on as it requires standing on one leg at a time or controlled movements if sitting.

8:30am - 12:00pm: Transportation to whatever the day entails (work, leisure, gym, etc.) can be difficult, since driving and walking may no longer be an option due to the severity of tremors, dyskinesia, body stiffness, and slower reaction times. Social interaction is also limited as a result of the severe slurring of speech and faintness of voice, often making it difficult to understand what is being said. Walking through confined spaces such as small hallways and doorways present optical challenges and are difficult to maneuver for those with PD, resulting in multiple delays from legs freezing up and refusing to move. Remedies for this include drawing lines on the ground for a visual cue or using rhythmic beats as an audio aid.

12:00pm - 1:00pm: Lunch time! Same troubles as breakfast. Food may lose its taste as the loss of smell and taste are both common symptoms. Hopefully, clothing stays unstained for the rest of the day; it's not like Parkinson's doesn't already provide enough physical problems to feel self-conscious about.

1:00pm - 6:00pm: Consistent with morning activities from 8:30am - 12:00pm. The feeling of isolation from a lack of social interaction and difficulty being understood is one of the more frustrating things experienced by people with Parkinson's, especially if the individual is unemployed due to a lack of ability to work resulting from severe symptoms. This is similar to other diseases and illnesses, and feeds into the potential for other issues to arise, such as depression.

6:00pm - 7:00pm: Time for dinner. In line with breakfast and lunch difficulties, not to mention it is rather difficult or borderline impossible to cook. If eating out, hopefully no one at the restaurant publicly passes judgement and the waiter/waitress doesn't get mad at the mess left behind.

7:00pm - 9:00pm: Usually time spent in front of the TV as it is the least difficult activity available, however, it can be made problematic by cramps, aching muscles, and restless leg syndrome from sitting too much. Even using a laptop/cell phone can cause issues with small keyboards/screens and shaky hands. Sneak in a nap while watching TV due to being tired from an inability to get a good night's sleep as discussed at the beginning of this schedule.

9:00pm - 10:00pm: Shower and preparation for bed creates difficulties consistent with morning prep. It is difficult to clean all parts of the body thoroughly on a daily basis due to difficulties with balance, mobility, and flexibility. Sometimes, it can be a battle just to get into the shower as they are often small and confined spaces, which pose as mental blocks for those with Parkinson's. In addition, chances are the last medication taken for the day has worn off already (involuntary movements need to be minimized before attempting to sleep) so moving around is extremely difficult.

10:00pm: Lay in bed awake due to a nap that was only a couple of hours ago. Trouble getting comfortable in bed from another of the countless symptoms of Parkinson's - restlessness.

Bonus: 1:00am - 5:00am: Violent kicking movements and screaming due to hallucinations and bad dreams. Also, lots of tossing and turning throughout the night. Can result in not being able to sleep in the same bed/room as a significant other. That will be sure to help with getting enough rest for the day ahead… fun!

Hopefully with the daily schedule demonstrated above, you are able to get a sense as to how Parkinson's affects the average person diagnosed and how much more difficult life is living with PD. Adding in the fact that a person with Parkinson's will also have to remember to take medication every two to three hours makes things worse, as constantly checking a clock or anticipating the next time for medication is mentally draining. Some days prove to be much better than others in terms of mobility, pain, and effectiveness of medication, and there is almost no way of knowing whether a good or bad day is coming tomorrow. That can be extremely frustrating, especially if you have plans or a job.

With the vagueness in estimates and a significant difference between the number of people with Parkinson's and the number of people actually medically diagnosed, there has been a historical lag in research and development of medication. While a person diagnosed today undoubtedly lives a significantly better life than a person diagnosed 15 years ago, there is still lots of room for improvement. Unfortunately, this will not change until illnesses and diseases that are far more fatal and widespread such as cancer are cured, as focus and funding is concentrated in those areas, and rightfully so. However, this doesn't mean that being diagnosed with PD doesn't still suck (for lack of a better word).

There is currently no cure for the disease. The most significant and effective treatment is the use of levodopa, a drug that releases dopamine into the brain. It is a treatment that was discovered roughly 50 years ago, without much scientific improvement since, and struggles to mitigate the increasing severity of PD symptoms over time. Levodopa also creates a noticeable side effect known as dyskinesia, which is the involuntary movement of limbs, and is often confused to be a symptom of Parkinson's. Since it can be hard to function normally if your arms are moving uncontrollably, other medication needs to be taken to offset the dyskinesia. However, using levodopa helps individuals with Parkinson's function at high levels similar to the average person during the first 5 to 10 years following diagnosis, and is currently the best form of treatment that exists.

There is promising research for more effective treatments such as stem cells, but they are still far from being ready for commercialization at this moment in time.

I hope this has painted a vivid picture of what Parkinson's disease is, and how it has affected my father for the past 17+ years.

Chapter 2: My Childhood

In the next couple of chapters, I will share my upbringing incorporating all aspects of my life including education, relationship with family and friends, hobbies, work, etc. so that you understand my background and where I'm coming from. Only then will you realize what I have by talking to others, which is that no matter how different the context of our stories, we all experience a similar form of suffering and pain. Hopefully, you'll also see that a lot of what I've used to help me through these tough times will very much benefit you as well.

My story begins on June 8, 1990 at St. Paul's hospital in Hong Kong, the day of my birth. I spent the first five years of my life in a city called Tsim Sha Tsui, which is still to this day one of the more popular tourist areas for visitors. Other than vague memories and flashbacks that come to mind when my parents tell stories about my childhood, I do not have much recollection of these first five years. My parents were happy, close to family/friends, and life was good.

Then came a fork in the road.

Those familiar with world history may recall that Hong Kong (HK) was once a British colony stemming back to the First Opium War in 1841, in which China conceded the then empty, undeveloped island as part of its defeat. As they required more resources and adequate defence of the colony, China leased Hong Kong to the British in 1898 for 99 years, following the end of the First Sino-Japanese War. In 1995-96, with the lease close to expiration, there was increasing discussion and rumours that the United Kingdom was considering a move to return Hong Kong back to China. If you don't know much about the area or its politics, Hong Kong was a democratic country under British rule, and China is a communist state. This created a number of question marks surrounding the future of Hong Kong, ranging from the economy, politics, human rights, and even representation in major sporting events such as the Olympics. After much deliberation, the UK decided to return Hong Kong back to China on the future date of July 1, 1997 with the agreement that Hong Kong would become a special administrative region of the People's Republic of China under the "one country, two systems" policy and the HK's "Basic Law" mini constitution for the next 50 years. This is set to expire in 2047. A summary of the important points of the policy and constitution are as follows:

- A "high degree of autonomy" in executive, legislative, and independent judicial power
- China to be responsible for defense and foreign affairs

- Banning of China's central government from interfering in HK's affairs
- No official presence in HK for the Communist Party of China
- Freedom of speech, press, religion, and protest
- HK to participate in all sporting events as a separate country

As you can tell by reading the bullet points above, the cultural and political differences between Hong Kong and China were numerous and significant in nature, and there was a lot of concern from HK citizens that life as they knew it was about to change under China's rule. This led many HK citizens to consider potentially moving to another country within the British commonwealth, as Hong Kong citizenship allowed for easier inter-Commonwealth immigration. This friction proves to still be an issue to this day. There have been a number of violent protests in Hong Kong fighting for freedom, democracy, and independence, including the Umbrella movement in 2014 and the Extradition Bill protests in 2019.

This brings me back to my story.

With me being five years old in 1995 and about to officially enter the education system in Hong Kong, my parents needed to make a decision as to what to do. Either stay in HK and hope that things remain as relatively consistent under Chinese rule as it was under the British, or choose to move to a new country. After much deliberation, they chose to make the move to Vancouver, Canada to eliminate any uncertainty and guarantee a brighter future for me. The decision was made with the consideration that Canada is a member of the Commonwealth, has favourable social programs concerning health care and education, and was a common immigration spot for other Hong Kong citizens at the time. I can only imagine how tough that decision must have been, as both of my parents were born in Hong Kong and had to leave behind their friends and family - all because they wanted to do what was best for me. As I've grown up over the years, I slowly begin to fully realize the immense sacrifices my parents made for me.

We've returned to Hong Kong twice as a family since the move to Vancouver, and it has broken my heart both times to see how happy my parents were to reminisce with friends over dinners, visit landmarks, tell stories from their own childhoods, and see relatives. Even though the last time we were there was back in 2013, I still vividly remember both of my parents saying goodbye to their siblings and parents, not knowing when they would ever see each other again. Those tearful farewells are memories I will never forget, because I was the reason for them. While I couldn't be more grateful for where I live and the opportunities I have been provided having grown up in Vancouver, I wish I could go back in time and convince my parents to stay in Hong Kong, for the sake of their happiness. They said goodbye to all their friends, family, and life in Hong Kong, all for me. Both sets of my grandparents were born and raised in Hong Kong, as well as my parents, so they did not know anything about immigration or what it was like to get up and move to a place 10,250 km away. To this day, I cannot even fathom the thought of moving to another country where I hardly speak the language, and I am ten years younger than my parents were when we moved. Even though I don't currently have children, I'd confidently say that I would not do that for them.

But then again, I don't have to because my parents made the sacrifice to move to a place as desirable as Vancouver so I would never have to even ponder a similar decision myself. It's one of the craziest realizations in life; you spend your whole childhood unappreciative of the sacrifices your parents made for you to live the best possible life they could provide, and by the time you come to your senses, it's either too late, or you spend your adult years doing everything you can to repay them and make the sacrifices worth it.

This book is part of my effort to do just that. It is an attempt to turn the sacrifices Kit Ling Kitty Tse and Man Ki Joseph Cheung made into a legacy of helping as many people as possible. At its core, my parents moved to Canada so that I could grow up in a country that did not hinder the ability to pursue my dreams, and while those dreams often change due to external circumstances, personal interests, and life experiences, I feel very blessed to be able to have written this book and tell our family's story. That is not to say I wouldn't have been able to do so in Hong Kong, but as we already know, China has and continues to crack down on free speech significantly over the years.

Anyways, back to my story.

In 1995, we moved to Vancouver with my dad's sister (or my aunt) and her family. Moving with them made the transition much easier for us, especially since it included my cousin who is a year older than me and also an only child. I consider him to be my brother. They have been just as supportive throughout this whole journey and we are extremely fortunate to have them as extra caregivers who look after my father, even though this gratitude isn't expressed often enough (thank you Wilfrid, Aunt Agnes, and Uncle Jimmy!). By our nature, humans struggle with being dependent and requiring help, and it is embarrassing to admit to needing it. As a result, it's been difficult at times to demonstrate gratitude for the things others have done to help us. You're reading this in part because it's been so difficult for me to tell my parents how thankful I am for everything, that I had to write a book for them to read!

The first couple of years were a struggle, as it usually is

with most lower middle class immigrant families, but we always stuck together. When we initially landed in Vancouver, we spent several months sharing one car and a two-bedroom apartment, which equates to six people carpooling around and two families sharing one living room and kitchen. My cousin and I would alternate laying across the laps of everyone in the backseat and ducking our heads in traffic for fear of being seen by the police!

That was just the way things were, and part of the sacrifice of leaving everything behind to move across the Pacific Ocean. I spent ages 6-26 living with my cousin's family either right next to us or in the same apartment/townhouse complex. We even split a duplex at one point! Slowly, our families developed stability in a new country. However, it was very tough for our parents to make friends, as their command of the English language was competent but not great. They leaned on each other, and continue to be close with a limited number of other close friends. Again, this was another aspect of their sacrifices I only recently realized in my mid-20s. It's often difficult to make friends the older we become; in fact, we tend to lose touch with more and more people as we age. My cousin and I were different, since we were afforded the friend-making machine that is the school system and daycare.

We were settling in just fine in Vancouver. Life was starting to shape up, and look similar to the blueprint my parents had in mind when they made the decision to move.

Then came an unfortunate break during my latter years of elementary school that would change our family forever.

Note: Context from here moving forward for the rest of the book: my parents tried their hardest to shelter me from knowing anything that would make me unhappy growing up and even to this day, so the details that I have described are mostly from piecing things together and soaking up as much as I could observe/hear at the time. As you can imagine, self and situational awareness are two of the traits I consider to be my strongest because of this.

Near the end of grade 5 (when I was 10-11 years old), my father started noticing a bit of stiffness in his left arm. He initially shrugged it off, thinking it was a sprain or discomfort from sleeping awkwardly. During that time, he had tried many different remedies from ointments to creams to therapy, but couldn't shake off the weird feeling. As a family, we didn't think too much of it and I certainly didn't bat an eye as I was too young. After all, as I've come to learn, the older we get the more body parts that seem to randomly hurt for no reason.

However, over the course of the next year, the stiffness

never went away. In fact, it progressively got worse and started spreading to other parts of his body. As doctors continued to monitor my father's condition, they eventually diagnosed it as Early Onset Parkinson's Disease.

My father was 45 years old at the time.

I can't remember if my parents ever sat me down and told me directly about my father's condition or diagnosis. After all, Asian parents aren't exactly known for being blunt and direct with uncomfortable conversations. It's a cultural norm to pretend everything is okay and never show weakness. Maybe they did tell me, but I don't remember because it is common to subconsciously suppress bad or traumatic experiences. Either way, I don't recall the conversation, and I'm sure little Michael didn't understand the severity of the situation or what it all meant in the long run - after all, I wasn't even a teenager yet. Over the years, I have managed to piece together the fact that my parents were devastated by the diagnosis and my father was depressed for a while afterwards. These are both things that don't come as a surprise given the circumstances, but break my heart every time I think about it and envision what it looked like in the doctor's office and through the following months.

I spent the next couple of years not understanding what Parkinson's was and how it would affect my father. I was stubborn, young, and took the approach that ignorance is bliss. I would also try a number of things to fix it myself, including twisting my dad's arm every chance I had, in hopes that maybe if I broke it, sprained it, or bent it a certain way, something that was out of place would pop back in and the stiffness would go away. Again, I was young and naïve. It seems silly looking back on it, but it was obvious that my father's physical state was beginning to deteriorate and I didn't know what else to do.

During my last year of elementary school (12-13 years old), the BC School Board went on a teachers' strike, and having Asian parents, they were scared that it would happen again during my high school years causing me to miss a period of school. Not to feed into the stereotype, but education is definitely not something to be messed with in an Asian family! Since I had a background in Catholicism and had already been baptised at birth, my parents decided to put me into a Catholic high school called Saint Thomas More Collegiate. They were outside of the public school system umbrella and weren't as susceptible to teachers' union strikes. This would inevitably delay my embrace and acceptance of my father's condition, as I only knew two people when I showed up for the first day of high school in grade 8, since all of my fellow classmates in elementary school went on to a local public high school in the district. The high school experience can be an intimidating one for a shy kid with no friends, so all I wanted to do was fit in. Having a father who wasn't like everyone else's was definitely the last thing that I needed to share.

As my high school years progressed, my father's condition became worse and worse, to the point where it was obviously noticeable. Not being able to hide the uncontrolled movements made things difficult, as people would often stare and become curious. My father was unable to stand still without his arms flailing and his head moving constantly. Being a teenager who was unsure of himself as a person with a face full of pimples and lacking confidence all while trying to fit in, I leaned towards hiding my dad instead of addressing any potential questions. I gradually decreased the amount of times I had friends over at my place as my father's condition worsened, stopped offering friends or teammates rides home, and also answered questions about whether my dad was fine with a simple "Okay".

Now that is not to say that I didn't feel the sadness and despair of the disease. I spent countless days and nights crying in the shower or in my bed, making sure I did it alone so that no one was able to see me. I'm not going to lie and say it wasn't and currently isn't heartbreaking, especially going through unfortunately common Parkinson's checkpoints such as arguments about finances, no longer being able to work, hospital visits, depression, falls in public, driver's license being revoked, etc.

There certainly wasn't a shortage of events over the years that would make anyone cry. I would also spend an absurd amount of time playing out numerous scenarios in my head about what I would say when friends wanted to come over to what I would do if someone approached my father in public, just so I could be prepared with the proper responses to prevent any situation that could potentially involve embarrassment for my parents or myself.

After all, I was young and stubbornly thought that a man should never show weakness or vulnerability. Ironically, all that practice has trained me to not panic or be flustered to this day when the unexpected happens because I am almost always prepared for a potentially negative outcome. It is second nature for me to have already played out all of the possible scenarios in my head for every situation, big and small, from a crucial job interview to a first date to where I'm going to park at the mall. This is definitely both a blessing and a curse that can drive people around me crazy, just ask my fiancée!

I am also much smarter now and know that vulnerability is not weakness. It is the purest form of non-physical strength that a human can possess. Exposing your frailties doesn't repel others, but rather draws them closer to you. It's a motivating force that compels people to want to help in your cause. I'll talk more about this in later chapters.

Nearing the end of high school, I had tried everything up to this point to help, including praying every single night for numerous years that my father would somehow be rid of Parkinson's in exchange for everything that I had and would ever have. It was also around this time that we went from going to church every weekend, to every other weekend, to eventually not going. I've never had this conversation with my parents to ask why, but I suspect it was for the same reason that I stopped praying; we had lost faith.

I was angry that there was this supposedly almighty God who created all of us and had our best intentions in mind, but somehow decided that my father was going to be one of those who suffered from this dreaded disease. How did that make any sense? Why would God do that, and how did he choose who? What was the reason for this? There must have been a lot of people out there more deserving of this suffering than my father. After all, there's no shortage of bad people highlighted on the news every night. Why not one of them instead?

Now let me get this straight, I am not trying to criticize religion in any way. There are many benefits to religion and its abilities to foster happiness. Being part of a religion helps an individual create a more active social life by being part of a community, find a strong sense of belonging and personal identity, discover a meaningful life purpose/orientation, and enjoy a healthier lifestyle (as many religions ban the use of alcohol, drugs, other bodily harm). To this day, while I see a place for religion in the world and all the good that comes from it listed above, I still struggle to find an answer to the questions mentioned at the end of the last paragraph.

As a result, I remain a non-practicing Catholic.

Meanwhile, during this time, my father spent every waking minute either driving me to school, extra-curricular activities, sports practices, or working, while my mother also worked full-time and made sure everything was taken care of around the house. My father realized the years left of him being able to help provide for the family were limited, and decided to increase his workload in an effort to maximize the amount he could save up to put us in the best financial situation possible. I really wished I could have gone back to tell him to be more selfish and take time for himself to enjoy life, have fun, and travel the world while he was still capable of doing so. There are probably a lot of items on his bucket list that remain unticked, but I don't think he would have had it any other way.

My parents' financial sacrifices allowed for me to have a childhood that was everything a kid could ask for. We certainly weren't rich by any stretch of the imagination, but they made me feel as though we had a lot more money than we actually did. To provide context, my parents came from middle class backgrounds by Hong Kong standards. My mother's side of the family was lower middle class, with her father being a goldsmith and her mother a housewife. She has three brothers and two sisters (Hi Aunt Flora and Judy!). Something I want to stress that the rest of the world may not quite understand is that while Hong Kong has one of the freest economies in the world and is constantly near the top of the most millionaires per capita lists, a significant portion of the population continues to live in poverty. When I say lower middle class, I mean 5-6 people living in a 500 square foot, 75-year-old apartment with no HVAC system, washing machine, dish washer, or other luxuries that we in first world countries would consider standard. My mom's brothers eventually moved to Honduras to work with their aunt and uncle so they could send money back to the family, which they unfortunately didn't end up doing. Meals would often consist of instant noodles, sardines, rice, spam, and other large quantities for low price foods. This was very much normal for a significant portion of the Hong Kong population, yet my mother often bubbles up with happiness reminiscing about her childhood. It's funny how a lack of wealth can sometimes decrease your problems and increase your happiness.

It's all about perspective.

My father's family, on the other hand, was upper middle class. His father was a police officer and his mother was also a housewife. Their family lived in a slightly larger apartment, with marginally better amenities and food.

My father has one brother (Hi Uncle David!) and the aforementioned sister.

It's interesting to learn about the backgrounds and upbringings that both my parents had and to see how it has affected their personalities and characteristics. My mother came from very little, and as a result, she is tough as nails, gives 110% at work, keeps a tidy house, and is extremely competitive in everything she does. My father, and I mean this in the nicest way, is a bit of a princess at times, willing to spend more money for luxury, and accustomed to a comfortable lifestyle. This was very similar to how his father acted, from my observations as a child before he unfortunately passed away. I'd like to think that I inherited a combination of traits from both of my parents, even though my closest friends and fiancée would argue that the mix was more my father than mother, especially when it comes to being a drama queen!

Anyways, that was a pretty long detour to give you background into my parents' upbringings, but it's important to understand the fiscal sacrifices they made for me growing up. I almost always got anything that I wanted, whether it was the latest toy or clothing. I did quickly get to a point where I realized this was the case and tried my hardest not to abuse the privilege (I never wore much designer or brand name clothing), but at times I would let my youthful desires get the best of me (I owned every Madden, NHL, and NBA Live video game from a span of 1999 to 2010). My parents paid for every sport or extra-curricular activity that I wanted to join, as well as anything I wanted to do with my friends. The only thing they asked for in return was that I focused hard and did as well as I could in my academic endeavors. Being an Asian child, I was never expected to contribute a penny towards food, rent or utilities even though I didn't move out until the age of 26. What a blessing that was, to be able to save up as much as I could and get a head start on real life with minimal debt.

We were a regular middle-class family, but my parents never failed to provide me with everything that I wanted. It wasn't always exactly what I had wished for, but somehow it seemed perfect. We never went on fancy vacations to Europe, often ate Spam, scrambled eggs or sardines for dinner, and took public transit a lot, but my upbringing was truly a happy one. Seeing how hard my parents worked to provide for our family taught me to be appreciative of their love and sacrifices. Understanding the value of money has been one of the most important lessons they have ever taught me, and has helped to significantly shape my life for the better.

As I transitioned to post-secondary education at the University of British Columbia and my father's condition continued to worsen, it became impossible to hide. I subconsciously shut down my private life, even to my closest friends. There was a time where I didn't even talk to girls because I was afraid things would progress to the point where they would eventually get to meet my parents, in which case I wasn't ready for what would happen. I convinced myself that people wouldn't accept me because my father has Parkinson's, which is ridiculous when I look back on it, but seemed to somehow make sense in the moment.

Throughout the years as I continued to mature, I became even more aware of my surroundings and the resulting consequences of life, which only furthered my understanding of the severity of my father's condition and the lack of hope for things getting better in the future. At this point, not only were his movements slower and less controlled, he also started to fatigue quicker, fall occasionally, and have trouble driving. His frustration was starting to show, as he was beginning to have more bad days than good. Seeing this, I started to shut down, ate poorly, dressed like a slob, stopped being social, and did things that were mostly within my comfort zone. I was miserable and didn't have anyone I could really talk to, nor did I want to share what I was feeling. After all, I was an only child. Listening to sad songs and reading stories of heartbreak online became my therapy, akin to going through a break up. It provided me a sense of comfort that others out there were going through similar issues as me, and could relate to my feelings.

At the same time, I couldn't let it affect my studies, as I was well aware of the sacrifices that my parents made for me to be in the position that I was in. I did a tremendous job compartmentalizing, and ended up graduating on the Dean's honour roll list with a bachelor of commerce from the University of British Columbia. One of the happiest memories and pictures that I have is of my parents and I on my graduation day, with the photo being taken seconds after both of my parents had cried tears of joy. I will cherish that moment forever.

Post-university life was much the same for me. To be honest, the years in this stretch jumbled together. It doesn't help that time seems to only speed up as you get older. I was becoming more aware of the situation with Parkinson's and my dad's deteriorating condition, all the while trying to not let it affect my work and career advancement. I was still very guarded regarding many details or information about my personal life and my father, but at the same time, I started to understand that it was holding me back and I wasn't going to be able to live freely if I continued to let Parkinson's dictate my life.

My father unfortunately didn't have the option, but I certainly did.

Eventually, I decided to openly share my father's story.

Chapter 3: The Breaking Point

When I graduated from university, I was fortunate enough to land a job at an accounting firm called KPMG. If you or anyone you know is an accountant, you're probably familiar with the grind of public practice (audit). I must say, it definitely isn't for everyone and I figured out within two months of starting that I wasn't going to be there for the rest of my career, but the three and a half years I was at KPMG also ended up being the most influential years of my existence so far. That time literally changed the trajectory of my life. Without them, this book wouldn't exist.

Let me explain.

I spent almost all of those years at KPMG around like-minded business people, as I filled the majority of my waking hours either at work or studying to become a Chartered Accountant. If you're unfamiliar with public practice, it's mostly just working 10-12-hour days followed by roughly 15 hours of schoolwork per week in order to achieve your designation, so I didn't have much time otherwise. In addition to that, there are numerous stages of vetting before getting a job at one of these accounting firms, from requiring an accounting degree to multiple rounds of interviews in which the success rate for applications to just get an initial interview was far less than 50%. All my life, I was used to being one of the smartest people in the room. In high school, I had a GPA of over 90% and made the honour roll every year. In university, I graduated with honours on the Dean's list. This was definitely something new I had to get used to... I was no longer a big fish in a small pond.

In fact, I was hardly even plankton.

During this time, I was introduced to a multitude of things in the business world that piqued my interest including investing, self-help concepts, real estate, entrepreneurship, the corporate rat-race, books, podcasts, etc. These are topics and concepts that I had never given much thought into, even though I graduated university with a bachelor of commerce. Given my shyness and desire to fit in, I did everything I could to catch myself up to speed on these topics so that I could engage in conversations and make friends at KPMG.

There's a commonly used principle created by famous motivational speaker Jim Rohn that would sum this up perfectly:

"You're the average of the 5 people you spend the most time with." [20]

I started to become more and more interested in certain topics such as investing and entrepreneurship. Right around that time was the beginning of the e-commerce boom and Amazon was becoming a mainstream platform. Entrepreneurship was extremely popular and everyone had some type of side-hustle or business idea. Of course, this wasn't the case, but as I was only surrounded by business-minded people, it certainly seemed like it. As a result, I was motivated to start something myself. Not quite sure what it was going to ultimately become (and to this day, I'm still not sure what the end result will look like), but I knew from reading numerous articles and advice that it needed to be something in a field I was passionate about.

One of the hardest things to do for most people is to make an extensive list of passions. Try it right now; I bet you can't list more than five things you are truly passionate about that you would spend 50-100 hours per week pursuing. As I was making my list, the one thing I never expected from the exercise was an increase in the understanding of who I was as a person. I thought about my hobbies, the sports I played, what I liked to do in my spare time, TV shows that interested me, my possessions, dreams and fears, what I consumed my time with, my friends, and everything else I could think of that helped to define me as a person.

What I realized from this was that the one thing I was most passionate about also happened to be my greatest insecurity. It can be weird to think of your insecurities as your passions, but as defined by Merriam-Webster's dictionary, passion is an emotion or "the state or capacity of being acted on by external agents or forces".[4] Therefore, an insecurity that affects your decisions is defined as a passion. For the average person, there is not a bigger external force that affects their actions more than insecurity or fear.

For me, this was my father's Parkinson's… and suddenly it all clicked.

I had been living under its shadow since the day my father was diagnosed, with the disease both consciously and subconsciously affecting every decision I made. As I mentioned previously, I was afraid to offer car rides to practices/games for teammates, ask girls out, invite friends over to my house, introduce people to my parents, etc. Simply put, I was afraid to live. That is why suppressing your insecurities is so dangerous; it ends up consuming your life, sometimes without you even realizing it.

Parkinson's was and still is to a certain extent an extremely uncomfortable subject for me to discuss. People could see that there was something different about my dad, but I never actually told anyone about my father's disease until I came out with my story. Looking back, I am not sure why. Maybe it was not wanting others to feel sorry for me, or perhaps it was because if I didn't openly acknowledge it, then it didn't exist. I simply never took the time to analyze why I behaved the way I did until I started my business idea. It has been the most freeing and rewarding journey of my life, and one that I will continue until the day I die. Even as I write this book, I continue to discover more hidden emotions and memories that lead to a better understanding of who I am.

Whilst trying to decide upon the type of business to create, I identified the biggest barrier in my path. Whatever business idea it was, it would be predicated on raising funds and awareness for Parkinson's Disease, which would require me to tell my story. The thought of this still gives me chills. I had never before even told anyone that my father had PD - how on earth was I going to sit down and put my story into writing!

After pondering it for a couple of months, I was finally in a state of mind mentally to truly reflect on my life and thoughts/feelings surrounding my father's diagnosis. Looking back, I am disappointed that it took until the age of 26 to confront my biggest insecurity so that I could turn it into a positive and live a life free of self-inflicted constraints. However, I also understand that many people live their entire lives never getting to this point, and as a result are never free from their self-doubt or circumstances. Self-awareness and reflection are some of the most important things you can do on a regular basis.

If you're not happy, dig down deep into what is holding

you back from the things you want and face them head on. It won't be easy, but it will all be worth it in the end.

It must be quickly noted that throughout this whole process, I had never asked for my father's permission or blessing. This is not because I didn't care about what he thought, but rather because Parkinson's had already influenced too many of my decisions up to that point. I wasn't about to let anything or anyone stop me from doing what I felt was right, and that was to turn a negative into a positive and raise funds and awareness for the disease. As a result, you've probably noticed that there aren't actually too many details about my parents' lives, other than the necessary ones to fill out my own story.

Another thing I had to consider (and you will too at some point if you decide to act upon your own misfortunes) was the point of no return. I had come across an article in Sports Illustrated talking about former NBA player Brian Grant's Parkinson's Disease diagnosis, and his decision to go public with it in an effort to raise funds and awareness.

Grant searched out Michael J Fox for advice, and Fox's response was: "If you don't want to do the advocacy thing, that's O.K… because once you step into that arena, you're in it. There's no stepping in and stepping out." [5]

In no way am I comparing my public profile to Brian Grant or Michael J Fox (I would have to be the most egotistical person ever!), but it was something that I had to think about. If I were to go public with my family's story, I would forever be known as the Parkinson's disease guy. Was this something I wanted? What if I changed my mind a year from now? Ten years from now?

Ultimately, it was a no brainer. I concluded that even if I decided to be an advocate for only a couple of months, every little bit of awareness and money raised would be better than if I had done nothing. After all, this wasn't about me - this was for my father and everyone else suffering from Parkinson's, and to give meaning to an unfortunate break.

The crafting of my story started, weirdly enough, on a flight back home from Windsor, Ontario having just attended the wedding of one of my good friends from high school. It was a date that I had circled for a long time in my calendar. I knew the travel between Vancouver and Windsor (an approximately five-hour flight) was going to be a time where there would be no distractions that would stop me from beginning to craft my story. Up until that point, I had decided upon the idea of finally telling my story, but put it off on several occasions with made up excuses. It ended up working to perfection as there weren't enough seats in a row for our entire party to sit together on the plane back, and I was left rows behind by myself with strangers.

Beginning to type out words onto my phone was no simple feat. This was the first time I had ever paused to reflect on my emotions and truly think about PD's effect with no distractions or interruptions. I had done such a good job of deflecting and compartmentalizing that I had managed to live most of the time never giving it much thought. I would still cry occasionally, but that's the beauty of defense mechanisms, they're there to protect you from sadness and pain. Sure, I was more than aware of my father's deteriorating state over the years, but I was also too busy trying to occupy my time with distractions so that I'd never have to ponder a problem that I couldn't find a solution to. After all, what is the point in thinking about a disease that there is (at the time of this book's publishing) no cure for?

As I sat there in the middle seat in between strangers on the five-hour flight, I began to pour my heart out into my phone's notes app, writing endlessly and only taking pauses in between to wipe away the tears. Of course, I was also periodically looking around to see if anyone was filming this maniac having an emotional breakdown on the plane for what appeared to be no reason. I wasn't even sure if half of what was being written even made sense. In a way, it didn't need to - I was expressing everything that had been trapped inside of me for the past 10+ years, and I could feel that every word being written was freeing me from my self-inflicted shackles. After about 2.5 hours, I had to stop. I was out of places on my sleeves to wipe away tears, emotionally spent, and needed a nap.

But I finally had a rough draft of my story! Much to my surprise, there wasn't much that needed to be edited. When it comes straight from the heart, there usually isn't any confusion as to intention.

Below is the final version of the first time I shared my story with anyone, posted on the website of the initial business idea I had to raise funds and awareness for PD:

Welcome,

Thanks for visiting. I figured I'd put a little something together to provide a premise as to why I started Tea Parky (including how it was named) and why a portion of all sales are donated to Parkinson's Disease.

First off, if you don't know what Parkinson's Disease (PD) is, please click this link.

All in all, the disease currently affects approximately 10 million people worldwide, which is more than the combined number of people diagnosed with multiple sclerosis, muscular dystrophy and ALS.

So, how does this affect me?

My father was diagnosed with PD around the age of 40 when I was 10-11 years old and has had the disease for over 15 years. It is extremely uncommon for a person to be diagnosed so young, as the average age of diagnosis is 62, and only 4% of people with PD are diagnosed before the age of 50.

Growing up, I always saw it as an embarrassment. I would pray every night that the disease would go away and things would be normal again. I used to think it was unfair for me to have a parent with PD. Everything was about me. As the years have passed, I'm left to wonder why it is fair for someone with still so many goals, ambitions and adventures to be diagnosed so young. It's frustrating beyond comprehension, even if my dad has made an effort to never show it when I'm around. Never once has he ever complained, no matter how bad things are. It is tough to watch a parent struggle at times with the most basic tasks that we take for granted on a daily basis.

Sometimes there really isn't much to do other than cry, and cry a lot.

Today, I realize just how ignorant I was back then, no matter how much pain my family has incurred. It is the single biggest blessing to be able to see life the way I do, and I wouldn't be who I am today without going through this.

Only recently did I start to talk about this, and it is still a rather uncomfortable subject for me. As I started opening up, a good friend of mine noted that stuff like this is the reason why he doesn't believe in God. After all, if there is a God, why would things like this happen? I give that question a lot of thought every single day. I don't know why bad things happen to good people. I don't know why the man crossing the street is blind, or why children are born with life-altering disabilities, or why homelessness and world hunger exist. It's kept me up many nights thinking about how some people have it so much harder than others. Life is frustratingly unfair like that, but I'd like to think it's so that we become more appreciative of what we have and in turn try to help out others who are less fortunate. I've come to realize that life is not about monetary possessions or traveling the world or watching your favourite sports team win a championship. It is about your impact on others, and how you are able to help those around you. It sucks that my father has PD. But if I am able to turn around and help even 2 people live a better life because of this, I'd like to think that it makes things a little easier to accept, and gives it a positive meaning.

This letter isn't about "poor me" or "feel sorry for me". So far, in my 26 years, I've been blessed beyond belief. Going through this only helped me develop the greatest appreciation of life itself. Instead, this letter signifies that it is time to get to work. I may be naive to think starting a website in my bedroom will make a difference. After all, I'm not a scientist, this isn't a Hollywood movie, and not everything has a happy ending. But if I am able to raise even $5, we will be $5 closer to finding a cure. And every penny counts.

Or perhaps, you have been personally affected by another disease or illness and would like to contribute towards that cause instead after reading this. I understand that PD is not as immediately life-threatening as cancer, and does not affect as many individuals as other diseases. But PD is what I am affected by personally, and as a result is what I choose to fight against. The truth is, everyone has a story that will break your heart. It is important to use that as motivation to take action. Hope is simply not a strong enough strategy.

As Chuck Klosterman puts it, "there is nothing scarier than thinking everything in life happens by chance." I'm a fond believer that everything happens for a reason, and this is my purpose. I've grown up realizing that sometimes life isn't fair, and as much as it sucks, you can either complain for the rest of your life, or you can do something about it. Not everything that happens to me will be my fault, but everything certainly is and will always be my responsibility. I sincerely hope you will join me in the pursuit of a cure for Parkinson's Disease.

My ultimate goal is to raise awareness about PD in the hopes that those who are currently affected by it are able to achieve a greater standard of living, and that eventually we will find a cure.

And if you currently suffer from PD, in the words of Jim Valvano, "Don't give up, don't ever give up." Keep fighting and continuing to be an inspiration to others. My father is easily my biggest hero. After all, there was and still is no explanation, no answers. And you're supposed to just accept it. You're supposed to live with it. He got cheated out of life itself, yet has never complained once. I don't think I will ever fully comprehend how much strength/courage that takes and the impact that has had on my life. And my mother couldn't exemplify the wedding vow "in sickness and in health" any more courageously. The love she shows for my dad is something that I admire and strive to replicate everyday towards others. I honestly couldn't have asked for better role models. Throughout my entire life, they've sacrificed their happiness in order to ensure I would never have to sacrifice mine, and now I spend every waking moment trying to pay them back. I wish I could give them the world. Again, I've been blessed beyond belief.

In conclusion, I'd like to end with this quote:

"If something is important enough, even if the odds are against you, you should still do it." - Elon Musk

Some people go through life never finding the one thing they're truly passionate about, whether it be a job, a person, an idea, a hobby, or a place. If you're ever lucky enough to find it, please pursue it with everything you've got, for all those who wish they did or still could. Finding a cure may take 5 years. It may take 25 years. Or it may even take 225 years. In fact, there's a chance we may never find a cure. But I'm only 26 and I will fight this thing for as long as I live. I've simply lost too much.

It is time to get to work, and to turn an unfortunate break into the biggest blessing of my life. #BeatParky

Thanks again for reading. ☐

With my story crafted, I launched my first business idea on April 17, 2017.

When I first launched the website and shared it through my various outlets to friends and family, I was extremely nervous about what people would think and say. I didn't want people to feel sorry for me, nor did I want my dad to be embarrassed. After all, I had never asked my parents for permission and didn't give them any advanced notice. However, the outpouring of support was overwhelming. I know it's such a cliché thing to say, but I was truly blown away by the amount of people who reached out, purchased products, or made donations. Telling my family's story has been the greatest decision of my life, and hopefully I've convinced you to do the same.

There is so much value in doing so, with minimal downside.

If not, let me present a famous quote from Steve Jobs that describes my perspective better than I could ever put into words:

"When you grow up, you tend to get told that the world is the way it is and your life is just to live your life inside the world. Try not to bash into the walls too much. Try to have a nice family life, have fun, save a little money. That's a very limited life. Life can be much broader once you discover one simple fact: Everything around you that you call life was made up by people that were no smarter than you. And you can change it, you can influence it… Once you learn that, you'll never be the same again." - Steve Jobs

You have been given the unique gift of the ability to share your story and influence the world for the better. It would be a shame to let it go to waste.

About two years later, I shut down the business and pivoted into other business ventures. Similar to the majority of other entrepreneurs/businessmen, I'm on to my next adventure in the constant search for an idea that

I enjoy executing everyday while maximizing my strengths. Tea (and the many different flavours of it) simply wasn't my passion, nor was I eager to become knowledgeable enough about it in order to succeed. Since then, I have tried a multitude of ideas including writing a book (which you are currently reading!), starting a podcast, hosting bar fundraisers, creating a blog, bookkeeping, and even making an online communication service. All in the quest to #BeatParky!

However, Tea Parky will always hold a special place in my heart, as it represents the leap I took to finally make something of the hand that my family was dealt.

Thank you to all who of you supported it

Chapter 4: Courage to Tell Your Story

If you have yet to tell your story and want to work towards doing so, this chapter is for you! As you can see from my story, there is lots of value in sharing your journey and experiences. They help to improve not only the lives of loved ones currently suffering, but also strangers who are affected by the same diseases as well. There is literally no valid reason not to share, and help us get closer to finding a cure for all of these maladies.

What are you waiting for?

We'll start by dissecting all of the reasons why you have yet to do so. Only by pinpointing the obstacles first can we then work towards overcoming them.

First of all, let me say that I totally understand. Afterall, you just read about how it took me over ten years following my father's diagnosis to be comfortable enough to share my family's story. There were a number of reasons why it took so long. This chapter is an effort to help you get over some of these barriers, having gone through them myself.

Below is a list that will be fairly familiar to you, and there is definitely no shame in any of these:

- **Embarrassment:** The majority of us have a desire to fit in - people rarely want to stick out or be different. Thinking back to high school or university, we often feel shy or embarrassed when we are forced to speak in public or are singled out for our differences. Sharing your story would be no different.

- **Not Wanting Pity:** A common human condition (especially evident in men) is not wanting to show vulnerability because it can be viewed as weakness. Our self-esteem is usually hurt when we must rely on others. The most common example used is not wanting to ask for directions when we are lost. As a result, it is our subconscious impulse not to ask others for help or to share any stories that show weakness and invite feelings of empathy. We simply don't want others to pity us because they feel bad about our circumstances.

- **Feeling Like No One Will Care:** In the age of social media, people tend to overshare personal aspects of their lives on the internet to the point where it becomes overwhelming and even irritating. Having read that, you probably just thought of that person (or people) you follow on Facebook or Instagram who shares way too many baby photos, random quotes, food pictures, etc. When we come across these posts, we usually scroll right past them and get annoyed. Sometimes, we even feel anger or hatred when a certain threshold is reached. At the same time, we crave social acceptance as humans and often find it through interaction and likes on our social media posts. Therefore, we become scared that we are posting something no one cares about and will not support/comment/like.

- **Not Sure How:** Wanting to tell your story but not sure which platform to use, how to do it, or where to even start in figuring out the answers to these questions. This one is common, but by far the easiest barrier to overcome.

These are all be significant obstacles individually, and in combination can definitely be more than enough to stop you from wanting to share your story. How you overcome them is largely based on your individual mindset and situation. Nobody can figure it out for you, and the timeline for each person will differ. There is no blueprint for this. What I can share is just from my own personal experience. I got to the point where it was impossible for me to stay quiet due to a couple of reasons:

- **The World Doesn't Revolve Around You:** When you break it down, being too afraid to tell your story for the reasons above or any other reason imaginable is awfully selfish. I got to the point where I realized that there will always be more good than bad that comes out of telling my story. Even if you only get through to one person and raise $0.01, the smallest amount of awareness and funds will always beat nothing. Here I was worried about my personal image and popularity while my dad and millions of people out there suffered from a terrible disease. He was embarrassed on a daily basis because of his uncontrollable movements, had trouble with simple everyday tasks, and was robbed of a sizable chunk of his life, yet I was too ashamed to share his story because I wanted to fit in and not want people to feel sorry for me. How stupid and selfish does that sound? We all have a duty to do what we can to help those in need, and prevent others from being in the same unfortunate predicaments in the future.

- **Everyone Suffers:** Whether it's diabetes, cancer, Alzeheimers, miscarriages, autism, etc., everyone has some form of a story you've been afraid to tell. That doesn't mean your suffering sucks any less, but it also doesn't make you special. Sharing will encourage others to do the same, which will raise awareness and funds, increasing the standard of living for all those who are currently affected by illness/disease, and push us that much closer to finding a cure. You have the power to do that simply by opening up!

-   **There Is No Wrong Way:** If you're hesitant to tell your story because you don't know how to do it, you've got to come up with a better excuse than that! In this day and age, there are hundreds of different outlets for you to share your story with the world. Also, our computers and phones have this fancy function called copy and paste, so you can literally share the same story across multiple platforms. If you're unsure where to post, why not put it everywhere? After all, what do you have to lose? Popularity? Don't flatter yourself - you're not more important than raising funds and awareness to help those in need. Besides, most of the ways you can think of sharing are free!

Hopefully after reading this section you have now been convinced to step out of your comfort zone and communicate your story! Of course, there is no rush to do so. Everything happens in the appropriate time and circumstance. I just hope you are able to see that the positives in telling your story will far outweigh the negatives. Take the leap, and remember who you're doing it for.

You'll be wondering why you didn't do it sooner.

Chapter 5: Concepts

Now that you've read about my life story, it's time to explain the seven concepts that I've learned to identify and appreciate through this journey so far. That's not to say that it's made the moments easier to experience or accept, because the level of sadness and suffering never changes. However, they've helped me turn an unfortunate break into a blessing, and given me a chip on my shoulder to use what I've experienced and provide a positive contribution towards society. I am confident in saying they will help you to do the same. We may not be able to control the disease, but we all have the power to decide our response to its effect on us.

The format of each of the following chapters will consist of the following:

- Definition of the concept
- My family's stories with Parkinson's and where I noticed the life lessons to be evident
- What I've learned and how I plan on incorporating it to better my life or the lives of others going forward

These seven concepts are in no particular order and I hope that you realize they aren't necessarily specific to a story involving Parkinson's. These relate to a lot of different forms of misfortune. In fact, not all of them are positive or happy-go-lucky. This doesn't mean we can't try to look at everything in a positive light, but at the same time we should be realistic and understand that a lot of things about our circumstances are just downright heartbreaking. I'm not stubborn enough to pretend that everything is always sunshine and rainbows when it isn't. The bad gives a sense of fragility and urgency, and helps us to truly appreciate the good even more. A bit of both perspectives at all times is important.

Now and again, it will be difficult to see given the circumstances, but I'm willing to wager that 100% of these concepts are present in every story. They're even in ones without misfortune, which I'm sure you realize by now are actually a lot more rare than you initially thought. When you do identify these seven concepts, everything changes.

It's also never too late to start looking. Trust me, I took over ten years into my father's diagnosis to begin.

Chapter 6: Empathy

The first of our seven concepts is the easiest to understand and relate to when it comes to disease/illness. It is almost instantaneously evident in everyone affected, and changes one's perspective on others. The concept is also a word that can be closely related to respect.

Empathy.

Empathy is the ability to understand another person's situation and feel the same emotions that they may be feeling by putting yourself in their shoes. In almost every case of the word being used, it has a negative connotation of feeling sorry for someone or showing pity. However, I don't use those terms because they provide a very sad outlook on life, which can be generally implied in cases of illness but never openly expressed.

This is the case for my family's situation. While we would never want anyone to feel sorry for us or show pity, it drastically improves the quality of life for those with disease if people are able to understand what they go through. In addition, it would also help increase the likelihood and speed of the discovery of possible cures as a result of awareness and funds raised.

You may be wondering why I am providing a definition for what appears to be an easy and commonly used word, but it is important to ensure there is no confusion as to the interpretation of this and all of the upcoming concepts. This adds more meaning to the stories and lessons below, and hopefully helps you better relate to events that may have transpired in your own story. As I've emphasized numerous times already, my journey isn't all that different from a lot of you reading, and sadly perhaps not even as severe or heart-breaking.

Merriam-Webster's definition of empathy is as follows:

"The action of understanding, being aware of, being sensitive to, and vicariously experiencing the feelings, thoughts, and experience of another of either the past or present without having the feelings, thoughts, and experience fully communicated in an objectively explicit manner." [6]

As you see, Merriam-Webster also does not make any reference to empathy needing to relate to a negative event or experience. Yet as a society, we tend to only feel empathy for those who are less fortunate, and end up jealous of others who we feel are better off than us.

We need to do a better job of celebrating everyone's success and working together to help improve the quality of life for everyone, instead of being in constant competition trying to tear each other down.

But that's beside the point - I digress.

This is one of the concepts in which stories and examples of where empathy is evident in my father's journey are literally everywhere and happen on a daily basis. Oftentimes, I view them as a sign of respect as well.

One of the more obvious ways that empathy exists is in the amount of people who go out of their way to help my father navigate his way around when out in public. Those familiar with Parkinson's disease know that walking through doorways is often a struggle as the door frame optically looks like a tight opening, and this causes people with PD to freeze up. The amount of times over the years I've seen strangers rushing to open doors for my dad and then patiently wait as he struggles to get through without asking a single question is in the thousands. In addition to the door example, there are a multitude of everyday things that strangers help my father with when out in public. Some of the more common ones include:

- Moving their chair in at restaurants so that my father can navigate his walker through tight spaces
- Getting up and offering their place to sit on public transit and at malls or other public settings

- Taking the time to understand what my father is trying to say as he mumbles through sentences with a soft tone

These are the things I think of when I ponder about empathy and respect; the understanding that someone is in need of help without explicit communication and the willingness to aid without hesitation or question. It warms my heart to know that as much as we see bad and evil things on the news, there are truly a lot of really good people out there willing to help try to make our society a better place for all.

In addition to strangers, I've received a lot of empathy from friends over the years as well. Even though I never openly talked about Parkinson's until a couple of years ago, it was pretty obvious given my father's involuntary movements and shaking that something wasn't quite right. There was no shortage of people asking me how my father was doing, and other questions of that variety. It truly meant a lot to me that people cared enough to inquire, even though I never shared any information with them. Those are the people and friendships that I will cherish forever. It's actually funny looking back on them, as there was almost an unspoken agreement that we both knew my father had Parkinson's (or something similar) but it was not to be talked about or acknowledged. After all, if I didn't say anything first, it probably didn't feel appropriate for anyone else to ask or mention it.

However, these questions and occurrences were one of the factors that led to me being comfortable enough to tell my family's story (I realize I've alternated between "my father's story" and "my family's story" about a hundred times throughout the book so far, but I'm not sure which one is more fitting and I think they're both applicable!). They helped me understand that we weren't alone, and didn't need to be, on this journey. There were many friends, family, and strangers out there who genuinely wanted to know if we were doing ok, and could relate our story to something similar of their own. This inspired me to overcome my fears and doubts about opening up. Eventually, it provided me with the courage to raise funds and awareness for Parkinson's by starting an annual bar fundraiser, to which I invited all of my friends.

The outpouring of support was more than I could have ever imagined. My first fundraiser was attended by 96 close friends and raised approximately $5K to be donated to a combination of three different charities/organizations (the Michael J Fox Foundation, Parkinson Society British Columbia, Rock Steady Boxing New Westminster).

(Photo Cred: Kushal Pachchigar)

I honestly couldn't even name 96 people I considered to be my friends before the event, let alone people who wanted to come and support my cause. If that isn't the epitome of empathy, then I don't know what is. I consider each and every one of these people to be family.

As I've said multiple times, I wasn't gifted with special abilities nor am I some motivational speaker or self-help coach. I am just an ordinary person with a story that isn't all that unusual, which is a sad truth to acknowledge. We all have the capabilities and tools to make a difference in causes that are near and dear to us, it's just a matter of finding that spark and acting upon it. The best part is that a significant portion of you reading this book right now are capable of doing things far greater than I can ever even dream of. My hope is that you will be inspired to do so!

In addition to that, there are also many ways that I will continue to use empathy in order to improve my own life and the lives of others.

One of them is volunteering. Empathy plays a significant role in volunteering - there is no personal glory in donating your time. We simply understand what others are going through and want to donate our efforts to the cause. 99.9% of the time, volunteering involves a direct or indirect effort to help improve the quality of life for the less fortunate. There is a quote that the President of South Burnaby Metro Club (a non-profit youth sports organization I've volunteered at throughout the years) found and eloquently said at our last volunteer awards gala to sum it all up beautifully:

"Volunteering is the ultimate exercise in democracy. You vote in elections once a year, but when you volunteer, you vote every day about the kind of community you want to live in." - Marjorie Moore[19]

Simply put, volunteering is the understanding of other individuals' situations and wanting to improve the society we're all a part of. Sounds very empathetic to me.

As I mentioned earlier, empathy led to my passion to raise funds and awareness for Parkinson's Disease. This includes organizing fundraisers, participating in roundtable discussions about fundraising, handling registration at the Parkinson Society British Columbia Superwalk fundraiser, and even donating a portion of net proceeds from the purchase of this book to organizations trying to find a cure or improve quality of life.

In addition to Parkinson's, I have also tried my hardest to say yes to every request for a donation relating to an illness or disease. Oftentimes, the donation is only $10, but it is hardly ever a no. Empathy has helped me understand that my father's story is not unique, and there are tons of people out there who are affected by other illnesses and diseases, and are just as passionate about their causes. In fact, a lot of people have it worse; I'm sure there are some reading this book right now who have a more heart-breaking story than my father's. We need to help support each other, and the first step is to truly understand what others are going through.

Empathy has also helped me rethink my perspective on life and made me a much happier person. There are many scenarios we encounter on a daily basis that provide the opportunity to be empathetic and appreciative of our blessings. A couple of examples below include:

- What right do I have to complain about exercise when my father would give anything to be able to move that freely?
- How do you stay a picky eater knowing that there are millions of people on earth (and thousands in your own community) who struggle to figure out where their next meal will come from?
- Wish you had the latest designer clothing? Make a trip to your local Salvation Army or thrift store and see how thankful people are to have quality second-hand clothing.

When you take a step back and put yourself in others' situations, you almost feel terrible for ever thinking of complaining at all. Empathy helps us to understand how truly blessed we are in our everyday lives, and not to take our lifestyles for granted. No matter what, there is always someone out there who would gladly trade places with you. Once you understand that, happiness and gratitude inevitably follow.

Last but definitely not least, empathy has taught me not to be assuming of others' situations. I no longer look at a homeless person on the street and think to myself, "why doesn't that bum just get a job?". Nor do I look down on individuals who resort to alcohol, drugs, gambling, or any other kinds of vices as escapisms to their current life. I realize that a lot of these situations occur as a result of factors that were largely out of their control or an unforeseen bad break, and that what we see on the surface from afar doesn't always tell the whole story. If it certainly doesn't with my father, I wonder how many stories and perceptions we assume about others are actually far from the actual truth.

Like the lyric from a song by Canadian rock artist Amanda Marshall, "Everybody's got a story that could break your heart." [21] Think twice the next time you choose to judge someone you don't know.

Instead, ask yourself what you can do to help.

Empathy is one of the most important lessons an individual can learn, and I am thankful it is one of the gifts that my father's unfortunate break has given me. It has changed my perspective on life and helped me become a better contributing member to society. This has in turn filled my life with happiness. Life is a boomerang and we get back what we give. The more we give, the more we get.

If you take the time to look for it, the lesson of empathy exists in your story.

Take a few minutes to ponder instances in which you've looked down on others and ways that you can be more empathetic to those around you.

Chapter 7: Luck

The second concept that this journey has helped highlight and emphasize is one that has many different interpretations depending on who you ask. In fact, a number of people don't even believe it exists!

That concept is luck, or lack thereof, especially when it comes to those diagnosed with an illness or disease.

Luck is not a difficult word to define. However, there are a wide spectrum of opinions as to how much influence it has in our lives to determine how successful or happy we ultimately become.

Let's define the word "luck" first. Merriam-Webster defines it as:

"A force that brings good fortune or adversity" [7]

and

"The events or circumstances that operate for or against an individual" [7]

I don't expect any ambiguity or rebuttal regarding either of the definitions mentioned above. Therefore, let's move on to the interpretation of luck and how much impact it has on our lives.

There are many conflicting views and quotes regarding luck and success. Some people say that hard work can overcome any circumstances and that you make your own luck, while others argue that the majority of our success is dependent on having good luck. However, I've noticed a trend in terms of attitudes, with belief in luck being tied to quality of life and financial comfort. It seems as though those who are below middle class or straddling the poverty line believe that luck plays a significant role into why they ended up in those situations, and not so much a lack of hard work, constant self-education, seizing opportunities, and taking calculated chances.

On the other hand, those who are successful and financially independent acknowledge that luck did have a role in their journey, but attribute its role to a far less significant portion than the first group of people noted.

It appears people have an inherent bias to blame luck for negative outcomes and are quick to pat themselves on the back for positive ones.

Before you get upset at me, I acknowledge that obviously there are going to be outliers. I am just speaking in generalities here. Clearly, it's hard to determine which group is right, as each individual case has unique circumstances and we can't replay the journey of life with different variables. Even if you believe in the simulation theory, we are unfortunately not at the controls!

As I continue on the adventure of my own life, my viewpoint on this topic has gradually changed. At first, I believed that luck played a significant role in an individual's success and happiness. After all, I grew up around an individual who I could see gradually diminishing through no fault of their own other than a stroke of bad luck.

As I mentioned before, there aren't any specific reasons why people are diagnosed with Parkinson's. My father didn't smoke, didn't drink, wasn't overweight, never worked on a farm or around toxins, didn't have an abnormal family history of illness and disease, and for the most part ate regular foods that the majority of the population eats.

Given our current scientific findings and knowledge, who else are we to blame for my father being diagnosed with Early Onset Parkinson's Disease other than Lady Luck?

However, I've come to understand that a number of baseline requirements need to be met before the element of luck kicks in and determines one's fate. Of course, there are lots of unique circumstances in which this is not the case, but the majority of people who attribute something to luck have not met these baseline requirements.

Blaming Lady Luck can come in the form of many differently worded statements that don't actually contain the word "luck" in them. They include:

- "Yeah, well her parents have a ton of money and just paid for everything. What has she actually earned?"
- "That guy was such a nerd/loser in high school."
- "If I was in that position, I could probably do the same or even better."
- "They get paid so much to do nothing at their job."

Oftentimes, blaming a lack of luck sounds exactly the same as jealousy. We're all better than that.

Anyways, back to the baseline requirements. During my time at KPMG as an auditor in my early years fresh out of university, I spent a lot of time immersed in the business world, picking the brains of many entrepreneurs while auditing their companies and asking them about their journeys. The number of stories and advice I received was truly priceless. You'd be surprised to learn how much people are willing to share with someone who wants to soak it all in and learn. After all, who doesn't enjoy talking about their own successful journey. At the same time, I was caught up in the rat race of public practice accounting, among hundreds of people roughly my own age who had huge ambitions and wanted to climb up corporate ladders as fast as possible. It was during these three and a half years that my perspective on luck changed, at least when it relates to wealth and business.

For those unfamiliar with the public practice accounting world, the structure of these accounting firms is a pyramid (no, not a pyramid scheme!). Every year, they would hire enough entry level staff to fill up the bottom layer of the pyramid, with the expectation that about 80% of individuals would complete the pre-requisites (educational courses and hours worked) needed to obtain a CA designation (Chartered Accountant, although it's now known in Canada as a Chartered Professional Accountant) before leaving to pursue alternative career paths.

We were all given the exact same blueprints, resources, and starting point, yet some became more successful than others. This provided the perfect observatory to see how much luck was actually an influence in people's success, especially since I was immersed in it with the same tools as everyone else.

I was able to conclude that external forces relating to luck indeed need to be present in order for an individual to achieve success in the context of the business world. However, the following two things also needed to be in place first, and they are both 100% in the control of the individual:

Hard work: Easy concept to understand. I mean, how many times have we seen successful people say this? Their stories always include a time in their lives when they worked 100-hour weeks, slept in the office, didn't take any weekends off, etc.

However, how many of us really work as hard as we can day in and day out?

At KPMG, I could clearly tell the difference between the individuals who were hard working and those who just put in the bare minimum effort. In fact, we had a saying for it:

"Do you want to be a boy scout? Or do you want to go the f*** home?"

Simply put, you could either do everything by the book and put in effort above and beyond the requirement, or you could do a good enough job and go home. The choice often wasn't difficult to make, especially since we were all consistently putting in 60 to 70-hour work weeks on average and not earning any badges. I definitely was not a boy scout, and those who were have gone on to become much more successful than I am in their careers. Success certainly isn't only defined by your career and how much money you make, but in this context, it's a solid measurement to gauge the effect of luck.

There is no alternative to hard work, and it is definitely a requirement in the likelihood of success before any external factors are present.

Lack of fear: Fear tends to hold us back from achieving many things in life. This isn't just relevant to the world of business or our careers, but also our personal lives. The fear of rejection stops us from talking to an attractive person at the bar, while the fear of others' opinions stops us from dressing the way we want or expressing our thoughts. Fear of failure keeps us from pursuing our grandest dreams and life goals.

In the context of the business world, fear relates to a lack of action regarding things that help our careers and trajectory up the corporate ladder. A fear of networking prevents us from making the necessary connections that open up opportunities for career growth and learning. The fear of failure stops us from taking on growth opportunities that are outside of our comfort zone. Fear of public speaking limits us from expressing our ideas, intelligence, opinions, and demonstrating our capabilities for larger roles at work.

At KPMG, there were ample growth and networking opportunities, but only rarely were these taken advantage of. In fact, during the networking events that we attended, the majority of us stuck with our cliques and never really branched out to talk to others present. After all, it can be uncomfortable and nerve-racking to socialize with strangers. Those who did were presented with a greater number of opportunities and ultimately became more successful.

These two concepts sound relatively basic and simple. However, the ability for an individual to be disciplined enough and avoid distractions that affect one's capacity to perform either function are far greater indicators to success than luck. We all have a more significant impact on our ability to achieve success than we think. At the end of the day, there's an inherent human bias to blame external forces for our misfortunes and to over-credit ourselves for the good in our lives. This is why accepting blame and criticism is one of the hardest skills to master, and one that is heavily emphasized by most successful people.

Despite this example being solely in the context of the business world, it proved to me that luck doesn't play as big of a role in outcomes as we believe or blame when things don't necessarily go our way. There are factors involved that are within our control, and they will end up being different when we compare the business world to personal hobbies to sports to health, but we need to identify them and make sure they are met before luck can play its part.

You may be wondering… how does this tie back to my father's story?

While luck may be an easy thing to blame for my father being diagnosed with Parkinson's, I don't think luck is as big of a factor in our lives as one assumes. As I explained above, we tend to push negative events towards external forces, but aren't as fast to credit positive outcomes to those same forces. Sure, it was bad luck that my father was diagnosed with Parkinson's, but at the same time, we were pretty lucky to immigrate to a country in which a public health care system exists and medication is heavily subsidized. If we were to move even just 150 km south of where we ended up (Vancouver, Canada) and across the US border, my family would definitely not be able to afford the amount of care and medication for my father, and there's a good chance that his quality of life would have been significantly worse. In fact, I'm not sure he'd still be with us right now.

It wouldn't seem fair to solely blame luck if we're not willing to give it as much credit when looking at the positives.

That is not to say bad luck didn't play a part in my father's circumstances, but rather that luck doesn't actually affect our lives as much as we believe. As we continue to learn more about Parkinson's from a scientific standpoint and understand its causes, the ability to blame luck diminishes since we can stop performing actions that increase the chances of inheriting the disease. Already, we are finding out that working in industries involving harmful chemicals, pesticides, toxins, and head injuries will increase the likelihood of developing Parkinson's. In addition, most illnesses/diseases are the result of unhealthy lifestyles or bad habits that we know are harmful to our bodies. Take alcohol, cigarettes, and lack of sleep as common examples. Therefore, we shouldn't be explaining away most things with luck, as it is not applicable in most scenarios. We should instead be assessing our lives and mitigating actions that increase risk. It's definitely a hard pill to swallow, admitting that a lot of our misfortunes are the results of our own actions.

Of course, it should go without saying that there are obviously many scenarios where luck is a significant factor, like in my father's case. After all, an identical clone of my father could have lived the exact same life and not been diagnosed with Parkinson's. No matter how hard we try, there are a number of situations in which the hand you're dealt puts you in a significant statistical disadvantage. Off the top of my head, where you were born and who you were born to are two of the biggest luck-driven variables in determining the success of an individual.

However, I think what most people have confused is the difference between luck and chance. I don't know if I can explain the difference as eloquently as a quote I came across from Chuck Klosterman, so I've decided to share it:

"Luck almost implies like a leprechaun or somebody is making this happen. In many ways, it seems like certain people are luckier than others. I think what that really means is that when they were given chances, they elected to pursue them, as opposed to step away from them. And that kind of creates the illusion of luck." [8]

Simply put, chance is being given an opportunity and luck is the willingness to take advantage of it. If you live in a first world country like Canada or the United States, there are no shortages of opportunities for each and every individual. By this definition, it is possible to not be successful if you were to be presented the opportunities but chose not to capitalize on them. Then again, you would see that as being unlucky or given the short end of the stick. Were you actually unlucky, or did you jump at the opportunity when temptation presented itself and failed to stay the course?

I think back to most things that I've failed at in life or considered disappointments, and I can almost always pinpoint something I did to negatively affect the outcome of the situation. It's definitely tough to accept responsibility for being the one to put yourself in situations of disappointment/sadness, but taking ownership and not blaming external forces (when it would be an easy cop-out) is the first step towards turning things around. The easiest example where this is most evident is in sports - often after losses, we're quick to blame refs or scorekeepers, but after wins, we talk about what a great performance our team put on. Be mindful not to only attribute external factors when things don't go our way, and only our own efforts when they do.

There are many scenarios, especially evident in third world countries, in which opportunities (or chances) don't actually exist. Now that is what I would call bad luck.

Changes your perspective, doesn't it? If you're still not sold, what choice do you really have? It's far easier to suck it up and live life believing that you have a far greater influence on the outcome - rather than constantly complaining about external factors you're convinced you can't change.

What a sad outlook on life that would be.

Given this understanding of luck's role in our lives, how have I made changes to better my own life and the lives of others?

As stated above, I have decided to accept responsibility for everything that happens in my life, and not blame any outside forces, people, or things that are not within my control. This has made me into a completely optimistic and happy individual. It's incredible how spiritually freeing it feels to know that you have the capacity to positively change any situation or circumstance because, after all, everything is the result of your own actions and intentions.

Does this mean that there are times where I accept responsibility for things that I know went wrong through no fault of my own?

Of course!

However, it's just a part of this mindset; you can't begin to put effort towards improving a situation until you've taken ownership and acceptance of it. I no longer spend excessive amounts of time worrying about things that are outside of my control or what other people are doing and how they may affect me. Being in a mindset where you are convinced your happiness is dependent on external factors is toxic and harmful.

Is this something I have to work on every single day? As with most things that are desirable in life, of course it takes continuous effort. Just like with exercise and education, consistency is key. But the results are well worth it, and more often than not, we learn to understand that many of the situations we attribute to bad luck or circumstance are actually things that we have the ability to make better.

Playing the pity victim card is never the answer.

I've also taken the effort to actively look for opportunities I am not currently taking advantage of in my life. The commonly used cliché is that growth comes just outside of our comfort zone. Knowing this, I actively assess situations and scenarios where I have been scared to do something, and look at it as an opportunity or chance to create some good luck in my life. This comes in a number of different forms, with the following as a couple of examples:

- Social events or networking opportunities in which I don't know many of the people attending
- Opportunities for side projects or to take on a bigger role at work
- Starting that business idea you've had for years
- Coffee to catch-up with an old friend or co-worker
- Volunteering with an organization in need of support
- Sub for a sports recreation beer league team because they're short players for a game
- Writing a book!

We can all recall times in which these opportunities have come up where we were either too scared to accept them due to social anxiety (after all, only weirdos are extroverts!) or too lazy to break routine and get off the couch. These could be the potential "chance" opportunities that are waiting for someone to take advantage of and get "lucky". Luck doesn't tend to happen for those who don't take chances (as Chuck Klostermann's quote mentions above), so actively audit the opportunities you continue to pass on regularly, and see if any are worth changing your behaviour/attitude for. Who knows? One of those chances could lead to you finding your soulmate, dream job, passion, happiness, or purpose.

I've learned in this journey so far that while my father has suffered bad luck, it isn't an all-encompassing term that we can use to explain everything that doesn't go our way. We have much greater control over the things that happen in our lives than we realize, and understanding this is a major key to achieving happiness and success in life. Take chances, always be prepared, show up on time, work hard, and be fearless. That is what creates luck.

As Monty Python made famous, "Always look on the bright side of life." [18]

Take a few minutes to ponder instances in which you've blamed external factors for things that happened to you. What steps can you take to begin accepting more responsibility for both positive and negative events?

Chapter 8: Regret/Appreciation

The third of these seven concepts is regret - or perhaps it's appreciation. But I'd say it's more regret. Actually, it's some combination of both, although I'm not sure what the percentage allocation of each is. It sounds weird to say, but these two concepts are intertwined and correlated to each other.

I'll explain shortly.

I would define regret as a negative connotation based on the sadness of not being able to do something that you wished you had done, whether it be due to money, bad decisions, external factors, physical limitations, fear, etc.

Merriam-Webster defines regret as "Sorrow aroused by circumstances beyond one's control or power to repair".[9] Again, we're bang on with the definition and how I interpreted the word.

Appreciation is being thankful and not taking anything for granted. It is being "in the moment" and realizing the beauty in everything.

I'm not even going to provide you with the dictionary definition of appreciation; there should be no ambiguity from my interpretation.

Let me first explain why regret and appreciation go hand in hand, to the point where I have combined the two into a single chapter.

Regret leads to appreciation. There is no regret if appreciation doesn't follow. After all, how can you truly feel sad about a missed opportunity if there is no gratitude for what that chance or moment could have been? Missing out on something forces an individual to be more conscious of their surroundings so as not to let it happen again. In doing so, you become more aware and appreciative of the blessings present.

My parents, being the stereotypical Asian parents, have kept many things relating to Parkinson's close to their vests in the interest of my happiness and not wanting to burden me with the troubles/pain of the disease. As a result, it has been extremely rare for me to see or hear them talk about many of the inevitable things that come with an incurable disease, such as regret.

One of the few times I have ever heard my dad talk about regret was in the midst of one of my career changes. I had been working at KPMG for roughly three and a half years, finally obtained my CA (Chartered Accountant designation in Canada), and got a phone call for a potential job in the biotech industry with an oncology company. After Googling what the word "biotech" meant, I was excited to move on to an opportunity that made me feel like I was making a positive impact in the world and helping others. In addition, the salary offered was a significant increase and would be the most amount of money anyone in my family had ever made. No, it wasn't anything crazy, just an upper middle-class five-figure salary that didn't start with an 8 or 9. But when you come from the upbringings that my parents had, this was validation for the sacrifices they made for me to live a better life. Heck, my parents were never granted the opportunity to even pursue post-secondary education because they needed to help their families financially by getting jobs right after high school.

When I told them I was accepting the job offer, they both were extremely excited for me. On our car ride to dinner, my father looked over and told me that if he didn't have PD, he could have helped me become even more successful. One of his regrets was that he didn't feel as though he was able to help me reach my full potential. I was extremely confused at that comment because currently I still don't feel like I'm anywhere near close to my peak capabilities, but looking back on it, I could see why he felt this way. After all, my father was diagnosed with PD when I was 12 years old, and tried to maximize his earning potential over the next 10 years while he was still physically capable of working. That would have spanned until I was approximately 22 years old, or just graduating university.

My mother was the one who helped me with all of my homework and really buckled down during my formative years to make sure I stayed on track - she cracked the whip when my report cards were less than stellar. It was easy to see how my father didn't feel like he helped much in my educational journey and the career path that I was taking.

Life outside of academics was the same way. My mother took me to most of my extra-curricular activities. She was the one who set the rules, taught me right from wrong, and made sure I ate all my vegetables. I was very much a mama's boy growing up, and still am. The regret he has is wishing he was more involved in helping raise me. This is ironic to me, because the lessons my father indirectly taught me through battling the disease have made me the man I am today.

This helped me realize two things. One, that my parents really had no idea how I felt about Parkinson's and the fact that I've actually turned out to be a more successful and well-rounded person from the lessons it has taught me growing up. Being in a family where my mom and dad never had conversations expressing their feelings to me, I found it difficult to do the same with them, even if they were happy conversations and ones of gratitude. It felt uncomfortable and embarrassing. This isn't just an exception in my family. After all, how many countless pieces of advice have we all come across that encourage us to tell our loved ones how we feel about them before it's too late?

In 2018, I finally decided to take that advice.

Although it was in the form of a note I had written out and left in my parents' mailbox before leaving on a two-week vacation, I finally found the courage to thank my parents and tell them how grateful I was for everything they had done for me.

The letter is below:

To Mom and Dad,

Over these past couple of years as I have matured, I have realized how thankful I am to have you two as my parents. As I coach more and more kids, I also realize the difference that good and bad parents can make in their child's future. For that reason, I wanted to write this letter to say thank you. I have also tried to translate it in Chinese as I know dad cannot read English too well, but it was done with Google so the grammar might be terrible! =D

I want to thank you both for the sacrifices that you made to move from Hong Kong so that I could live a better life in Canada. Only now do I realize how hard that must have been and all the friends and family you had to say goodbye to, just so that I could grow up in a better environment than you guys did.

Thank you for teaching me the proper values growing up. Thank you for teaching me to work hard and have good manners. Thank you for sacrificing your own needs to buy me every toy. Thank you for always pushing me to be the best that I can be. Thank you for giving me every opportunity to live the life I want.

I know you both want me to continue working in accounting/finance and live a safe and financially comfortable life. And I thank you for pushing me to work hard in school and get my CA designation, so that this choice will always be an option for the rest of my life.

However, you moved to Canada so that I could live a life of opportunity and freedom, and pursue my passion. I have always wanted to run my own company, and because of the position you have put me in, I can afford to try it and can always go back to accounting/finance if it does not work out. Both of your impacts, especially with dad being diagnosed with Parkinson's, has helped me to appreciate how lucky I am, and I want to help others who are less fortunate. That is what I think life is about and what brings me the most happiness. As a result, I have decided that sometime in the next 1-2 years, I will be quitting my job to open a coffee shop. It will be a place where I will have many community events, create jobs for people, hold fundraisers to raise money, and much more.

I have decided to name the business "Joe & Kit". I hope you don't mind. Logo is on the next page.

Almost every day, I think about how lucky I am. I didn't get to choose where I would be born and who my parents would be. I am so lucky to have you both as my parents. Without you, I would not be in the same situation. Thank you both so much. I am currently very happy with my life and excited about the future.

I hope I have made you both proud. I love you both.

I am too shy to say this in person, but I think it is very important for you to know.

Your son,
Michael

Thus, the origin of Joe & Kit was created. It has become the company name that I have used in all of my business endeavors moving forward. Although I never ended up opening the coffee shop, I did quit my biotech job to pursue more of an entrepreneurial role with a small business. Someday, I hope to become an entrepreneur. I am just waiting for an idea that feels right, and unfortunately coffee doesn't. Should have known after trying my efforts with tea! However, my parents understand that it is their sacrifice which allows me the opportunity to do anything I want with my life. The possibilities are literally endless.

All thanks to them.

The email they sent back to tell me how proud they are is something I will cherish forever - and no, we've never had a conversation about it since. This isn't some textbook fairytale story where all of a sudden I gather the courage and tell them in person after many years of neglecting conversations about feelings. That's not how life works. Breaking out of my shell to express my deepest emotions is a constant process that I am consciously working on everyday, and I understand that it will take time. It doesn't just happen overnight - the key is to consistently take steps in the right direction. Just like the advice that I said was cliché, if you haven't told your parents (or loved ones) how you truly feel about them, please do so before it's too late. It will be one of the best things you ever do in your life.

Trust me.

The second thing I realized when my father said he wished he didn't have Parkinson's so that he could help me become more successful, is that my parents had a far grander vision for my future and believe in me much more than I do in myself. It's given me the confidence and drive to pursue greater ambitions in an effort to make my parents proud. I've also become more aware and thankful for the opportunities to success my parents have paved for me, and strive to fully maximize the potential of every chance I come across. They certainly never had the same luxuries that they're giving me, and this is only the beginning.

Like I said, regret often leads to appreciation.

Another instance where regret and appreciation have been present is in my daily life, especially as I continue to get older. Moving to Canada has afforded me tremendous opportunities I wouldn't have had otherwise, but at the same time, these are experiences that my parents never had the chance to enjoy for themselves. As I come across these things in my everyday life, I try to take many pictures to send to my parents so that we can share in the experience together and they are able to live vicariously through me.

In a way, it also is how I show my appreciation for their sacrifices and to say thank you.

These common life events can be anything from dining at fancy restaurants, road trips, Christmas presents, curling, carving a pumpkin, or snowshoeing, etc. At the same time, I sense that these videos and pictures bring up regret in two ways:

- Regret that they did not have the opportunities or financial ability for these experiences.
- Regret that my father's physical state has prevented him from experiencing some of these things, and left a lot of items on his bucket list.

These are both extremely real regrets and I often struggle to find the right balance of sharing my experiences with my parents, but at the same time not making them feel regret and sadness. As the years progress, my appreciation of even the smallest things, has magnified. To provide an exaggerated example, it has made running half-marathons somewhat tolerable, knowing that my father would trade anything to struggle through 21.1 km. Comparing hard-ships in my life to his has helped me eliminate a lot of excuses and self-pity.

In addition to the letter I sent my parents, I have tried to change the way I live my life in the following ways after understanding the regrets my father has had as a result of Parkinson's:

First, I have made my best effort to include my parents in experiences that they still have the ability to participate in, such as going to fancy restaurants. They say "money can't buy happiness", so anytime that it can buy an experience or luxury that my parents couldn't afford growing up, I try my best to do it. Our opportunities to do so decrease with age, so I want to maximize the time we have left together. Money comes and goes, but memories last forever.

Second, I try to live my life with a clichéd "no regrets" mentality. Let's get this straight, as everyone's interpretation of that cliché is different. I'm not saying that I go out there with the "no regrets" attitude that tomorrow is not promised, and therefore I max out all of my credit cards and travel the world, jumping out of airplanes everyday. No, my definition of "no regrets" is to clearly define what it is I want out of life, and then make decisions to optimize the likelihood of me achieving those goals.

I don't want regrets when I am older from not accomplishing as much as I would have liked because I let short-term temptations get the best of me. As a result, I attempt to make more conscious decisions (especially as I continue to get older) about not sacrificing long-term, big picture happiness for short-term, temporary joy. This means not making impulsive shopping purchases, choosing books over TV, education instead of video games, and living more frugally in general, in the hopes of being able to achieve some of the bigger picture financial and life goals that I have.

A friend of mine once sent me this quote (and I wish I could find out who came up with the quote so I could give them credit but unfortunately my Google searches have been unsuccessful) that continues to drive this mentality into me every single day:

"Someone once told me the definition of Hell: The last day you have on earth, the person you became will meet the person you could have become." - Anonymous[17]

If that doesn't motivate the heck out of you to live a life of no regrets and maximize your potential while you can, you probably don't have a soul!

Who knows - maybe I do all of this and still come up short of achieving my goals. Life can really be unfair like that (just ask my dad), but I think I would be able to live with the results, knowing that I'd have given it my all and there wasn't much more that could have been done. That is my definition of "no regrets".

Third, I try to be as aggressive with my time as possible. Those who know me know that I lack patience. There are just so many things I want to do and accomplish in a limited amount of time that patience isn't something I appreciate. Since we don't know how much time each one of us is given, I tend to be meticulous about always having to plan my days and weeks. Every minute needs to be accounted for, which can be pretty annoying if you ask my fiancée! To sum it all up, I once came across the following quote shared by our head coach (did I mention I love quotes?) while helping coach a high school basketball team that I think is tremendously fitting for life:

"Potential has an expiration date."

When we are born, we have our whole lives ahead of us. The possibilities are endless and the sky's the limit. However, as we grow up, time seems to move exponentially faster and we are bound by more responsibilities (i.e. providing for our children and families) that limit our possibilities/options. In addition, our physical limitations increase and slowly eliminate our ability to accomplish certain things, sometimes faster than we initially predicted. Knowing that an expiration date exists but not being sure when that date might come drives me to push the limits and move as fast as possible.

At the same time, I've learned to understand that some things do take time, so it's about speed and urgency in the day-to-day, whilst still having patience looking at the big picture.

Last but not least, I attempt to cherish my experiences and memories as much as possible. Understanding that a stroke of bad luck may occur tomorrow that prevents me from doing these things helps me to appreciate them more, and document as many of them as possible while I still can. This includes taking an excess number of photos and videos for almost everything that I do. Our memories often fade and deceive us over the course of time, as they are heavily linked to our emotions. A photo or video will always ring true. In addition, I challenge you to perform an inventory count (there's the accountant in me!) of photos that you already have, especially with loved ones during cherished experiences. If you're like me or most people I have asked, you probably have a lot less photos with family and friends than you thought, and a surprising amount of food or other random photos.

You will also come across memories that you completely forgot about, and they will bring you tremendous joy.

Start taking more photos and videos that include yourself or with loved ones. It will decrease potential regret for not capturing or remembering the moments in the future, and help you to appreciate them more when looking back. Photos can always be deleted in the future, but you can't travel into the past and take them. I know it's worked for me since I started adopting this mentality. And best of all, photos/videos are free to take if you have a cellphone! You literally have no excuses.

Hopefully, this has helped you see the ways I've been able to use my father's disease to understand regret and appreciation, and how they both fit into my life. It has made me a much happier person.

As I've done many times throughout this book and will continue to do going forward, I'd like to emphasize that there is nothing spectacular or unique about my family's story. The majority of us are overcoming or have overcome countless hurdles to become the people we are today. I live a typically modest and average life, but in a way, sharing my family's journey has freed my soul and made me very happy. I'd encourage you to tell your story, and turn the negative regrets into maximum appreciation!

Take a few minutes to think and write down the many ways that regret has been evident in your own story. What about things you have taken for granted that you should be more appreciative of? What are some actions you can do moving forward to minimize regret in your life?

Chapter 9: Toughness

This next concept is a word that is used for literally anyone affected by an illness or disease, whether or not they show it explicitly. It is a requirement to fight through trying times, and endure the treatments required to stay alive or maintain a consistently comfortable quality of life.

This characteristic is toughness.

Contrary to most public perceptions, as well as the first thing that comes to your mind when you think of the word, toughness has nothing to do with physical appearance or how loud you can shout. It is a mentality and a state of mind. When I think of toughness, I find it easiest to explain with different adjectives that are used synonymously to describe someone who embodies the word. A few examples include:

- Resilience
- Strength
- Determination
- Struggle
- Perseverance

Merriam-Webster defines toughness as "capable of enduring strain, hardship, or severe labor".[10]

It's not hard, when thinking about my father, to come up with stories where toughness is present. I mean, it's literally in his everyday life, as people with Parkinson's struggle with most things the average person doesn't even think twice about, such as getting out of bed in the morning or eating using utensils.

Yet I can't remember a time when my father has complained about the disease, said no to an activity or event that our family wanted to do despite obvious physical limitations, or felt sorry for himself. Most times, he commits to things he knows his body can't physically do, especially as the years go by and the disease worsens.

This often results in situations where he almost falls or puts himself in scenarios where he feels publicly embarrassed; yet he doesn't care, because he doesn't want to let us down and have Parkinson's determine our family activities. My father has never been in a fight in his entire life, but he is the toughest person I know.

You can't tell me that this isn't a normal trait present in every single person fighting something. It's there in every story, I guarantee it. You just have to be looking for it.

There are a couple stories that come to mind when I think about my father's journey and the word toughness. One of them is going in to perform deep brain stimulation (DBS) surgery. For those unfamiliar with

DBS, it involves implanting electrodes into different areas of the brain that produce electrical impulses to help regulate and offset abnormal impulses. These impulses affect certain nerve cells inside the brain, and help Parkinson's patients with an increase in mobility and other functions. The stimulation is controlled through a pacemaker-like device that is implanted under the skin, with an electrical wire that travels from the upper chest into the electrodes in the brain.

The positive effects that DBS provides people with Parkinson's vary on a case by case basis (as almost every case of Parkinson's has differing degrees of symptoms), but needless to say, it is very much desired for most people affected. Luckily, living in a country with a publicly funded universal health care system afforded my father the luxury to be able to have the surgery done for free. As I alluded to in the chapter on the concept of luck, if we moved even just 150 km south and across the border into the United States of America, DBS surgery would have cost roughly $65,000.

Needless to say, it'd be a price that would have been difficult for our middle-class family to swallow, and we would have had the uncomfortably difficult choice between financial well-being and my father's quality of living.

Thankfully, we did not have to make that decision.

However, given the fact that the health care system was subsidizing this surgery and government budgets are often tight, there were a number of criteria my father needed to meet regarding years diagnosed and physician recommendations before he was eligible for DBS. Once eligible, he was placed onto a waitlist in which the wait time for surgery was not determinable as more severe cases were given priority and there was only one doctor in the entire province of British Columbia who was trained to perform the operation. Each one lasts roughly six hours, so combined with the doctor's research work, time off, and other endeavors, only about 30-40 DBS surgeries are performed on a yearly basis.

There is a need for funding to train future surgeons to be able to perform the operation, but in a publicly funded health care system with a tight budget, non-life threatening surgeries for a disease that affects a relatively small number of people who are mostly over the age of 65 are often put on the backburner.

As a result, my father ended up having to wait roughly 13 years after being diagnosed before having DBS implemented into his brain. Of course, his quality of life would have drastically improved over his current circumstances had he been given the surgery earlier into his diagnosis before the effects of Parkinson's started to wear his body down. However, given our family's lack of ability to pay for the surgery otherwise, we are very grateful that my father was able to have the surgery done at all. Although the improvements and differences aren't as staggering, it has still vastly helped improve my father's quality of life. For that, we will be forever thankful.

Now that you have an understanding of DBS, back to the story on toughness.

We only became aware about 7-8 years into the diagnosis that DBS was a possibility. After looking into the options and jumping through all of the necessary hoops, we were finally placed onto the waiting list and told to be ready at any time for a phone call in which we would be scheduled for the surgery roughly three to four weeks later. Years went by after initially being placed onto the waiting list, and as my father's condition seemed to exponentially deteriorate and his quality of life free-fall (for lack of a better word as he was now no longer able to work a full-time job or drive a car), we slowly began to lose hope and became increasingly frustrated.

While some may not think working or driving is that big of a deal, they are core essentials that provide opportunities for happiness and self-esteem. Driving provides an individual the ability to easily travel wherever they please and engage in social activities. Work provides things such as goals and structure, reward and recognition, a sense of identity, and social belonging. Unemployment is one of the most critical threats to a person's happiness.

Again, I want to state that we are extremely thankful to live in a country with a healthcare system that offered my father the ability to have this surgery at virtually no cost, but knowing there is a remedy to help improve his quality of life and not being able to access it for years is one of the most infuriating things I've ever experienced. I prayed the call would come every single day (back when I was still religious), but to no avail.

We were on the waiting list for approximately three and a half years when the call finally came. FINALLY! It was an extremely joyous moment, as we had been waiting for this DBS procedure since the first day we were introduced to it. From the time of diagnosis, this was literally the only beacon of hope to help mitigate and counter the slowly intensifying effects of the disease. As I've stated throughout the book, research and knowledge on Parkinson's is stagnant and out-dated, and there is currently no cure. Sure, it is awfully dangerous to put all your eggs in one basket, get your hopes up, and over-emphasize the positive effects of this one "saviour" surgery by only dreaming about the best-case outcomes of DBS, but what choice did we really have? My father wasn't going to magically get better, and DBS has a strong, proven track record, including high profile cases like Michael J Fox. Sure, Michael J Fox had DBS performed early on after his initial diagnosis, but it was working extremely well for him and it was hard not to be excited.

At this point, the measure of success was not high - anything would be considered an improvement.

As the day of the surgery approached and we were going through all of the pre-surgery info sessions and body checks, the moment seemed almost surreal to me. My father was finally going to have the operation I had prayed years for, and it would help to improve his quality of life. At the same time, it was also starting to make my parents nervous. I don't want to get too graphic in the description of DBS, but the surgery requires the drilling of multiple holes into the top of the forehead so that electrodes can be inserted into the brain. That image in and of itself sounds scary enough.

However, to make matters worse, only local anesthesia is used and the patient needs to be fully awake. Since it involves implanting items into the brain, constant communication with the surgeon is necessary throughout the whole process to ensure everything goes smoothly.

One miscalculated movement could be catastrophic. The thought of being awake while having two holes drilled into the top of my skull and blood gushing everywhere is more than enough to make me light-headed. My father was obviously scared, but determined to put on a brave face and get it over with, as he understood it was for the best. Afterwards, he would tell us that he could see the blood pouring out of the top of his head like a water fountain when they drilled the holes. My mother also worried about the whole procedure; however, she was determined to put on a strong face and be there for my dad. She knew only one of them could have doubts about the procedure, and it was never going to be her turn.

After what seemed like months and hundreds of pre-surgery procedures (when in reality it was about a week and two to three visits), the day of the surgery had finally come! I remember the day like it was just yesterday. Having taken work off, I drove my father into the hospital early in the morning around the break of dawn to go through all the day-of surgery procedures. The surgery was going to last approximately 6 hours. We dropped my dad off and proceeded to sit in the surgery waiting room. As it was so early in the morning, the room was empty and it was just me and my mother. Due to a combination of being half asleep and hundreds of emotions/thoughts racing through our minds, we were both very silent. Although we were briefed that the chance of the surgery going wrong resulting in death was only around 3-5%, it felt like a very real possibility to us.

It's crazy how your mind goes to extremes so fast when you incorporate emotions. My mom killed time figuring out sudokus and playing Candy Crush. She enjoys puzzles and games that involve using her brain, so this was the perfect distraction. In fact, she didn't seem phased - nothing ever phases her. That's my mom; the rock of our family. I, on the other hand, was trying to read a book but couldn't focus. I was an emotional wreck on the inside, playing through every possible scenario in which something could go wrong, but didn't let it show through to my calm exterior.

In a way, this fittingly explains our family's communication during my father's journey with Parkinson's.

About an hour later, a nurse came out to the waiting room asking for us to go and see the surgeon. A wave of panic hit us and my heart sank deeper than anything I had ever felt in my life before. The surgery was supposed to take roughly six hours and wasn't supposed to start for another 30 mins; why on earth did the surgeon want to see us?

We knew something was wrong.

Rushing through the doors from the waiting room into the operation preparation room, we saw my father in a hospital bed with the surgeon standing next to him. As we were moving closer towards them at a brisk pace, a sense of relief came when we saw that my father was moving and awake. Now the next question was trying to figure out what was wrong, but at least we knew he was still alive.

What ensued were the following words uttered from the surgeon to my mother:

"Unfortunately, we are unable to operate on Mr. Cheung today. The nurses had a mix up and gave him his medication this morning. The medication has made him far too shaky and it would be too dangerous to operate. We will have to postpone it to a future date."

As explained, certain Parkinson's medications help my father move. Having taken the medication, my father would have involuntary movements for the next 4-6 hours while traces of it were still in his body. Given what I had just explained about DBS surgery requiring drilling holes in the top of the skull, it would be far too dangerous to operate on an individual who could not sit perfectly still. In regular protocol, my father would not have had any Parkinson's medication starting around dinner time the night before.

I can't name a single moment in my life in which I experienced more sadness and disappointment than the 30 seconds following the conclusion of the surgeon's explanation. To no surprise, my dad was in disbelief and started to ask questions to the surgeon as to how this mix up could have happened. My mother was also asking the same questions and they proceeded to talk over each other, understandably in shock and anger. I cried like a little baby. We had waited years as a family for this day to come, did everything properly to prepare, and now due to a clerical error which led to the nurses giving my father his medication in the morning, we were being robbed of this opportunity. We later learned that there were no nurses at the hospital during that shift who had experience with Parkinson's patients, so they were unsure what to do and panicked. Just another one of the struggles of being affected by a disease that is relatively uncommon.

Back to the waiting list my father went, with no estimated timetable for a second opportunity. 'Frustrated' seemed like an understatement.

After getting over the shock of the initial moment and calming down a little bit (although we were in the hospital for another 15-20 minutes as my parents continued to express their displeasure at how an error this big happened so easily), we proceeded to leave the hospital and grab a bite to eat. After all, it was breakfast time and no one had eaten yet.

We decided to go to a restaurant nearby called Banner, which was a medium sized, ordinary family diner that had friendly faces and affordable prices. It had the feeling and aura of a Ricky's, Chili's, or Old Country Buffet. Sadly, it's no longer in business, but this was a flashback down memory lane. We used to go to Banner almost every weekend as a family when we had first moved to Vancouver and lived nearby. In fact, we even went there the first Christmas after we moved! Christmas in Hong Kong isn't quite the spectacle it is in North America, and my parents were surprised at the lack of stores and restaurants open on December 25. I have extremely fond memories of ordering the spaghetti and meatballs every Friday or Saturday night, and then getting a scoop of ice cream from the Baskin Robbins that was attached to the restaurant.

On that day, those same moments seemed distant and unfamiliar. As we sat down and waited for our food to arrive, the conversation circled around fate and destiny. My mom would say things such as "God has bigger plans" and "today just wasn't meant to be", desperately trying to see the positive in the situation. It was ironic for a family that wasn't religious to resort to explaining this situation with a higher power, but ultimately nobody really knew what to say. We were in shock. A day we had looked forward to for years had now become a nightmare.

The nightmare lasted about another six months after that, until the phone finally rang again and we got the call to get ready for DBS surgery. This time, my mom had made multiple calls and checks to ensure the same situation wouldn't happen again. To the credit of the hospital, they also ensured that there would be a nurse on that shift who specialized in caring for people with

Parkinson's. The operation went smoothly and my dad has some battle scars on the top of his forehead to show for it all, but it's the journey to get to that moment that tells you about my father's toughness. After breakfast at Banner on that morning, he has never brought up that day or complained about it ever again. It was just another bad break, albeit a significantly larger one, in his fight against Parkinson's. They keep coming in waves, and the waves seem more frequent as my father gets older, but he never fails to take them in stride and keep trucking along. The ability to do that knowing there isn't an end in sight and a cure probably won't exist in his lifetime is something that is extremely admirable.

Imagine running a race in which you knew there was no finish line. At some point, most of us would eventually quit. A few, if any, keep going. That is the definition of toughness.

Another example throughout this journey in which the concept of toughness has been present is when my father broke both of his hips. Although they weren't both broken at the exact same time, they happened within a one-year span and required my father to undergo hip replacement surgery twice. Broken bones are something that is common amongst people with Parkinson's, because of both the lack of coordination and mobility leading to more falls than the average person, as well as brittle bones resulting as a side effect of the copious amount of medication consumed. Taking

15-20 pills on a daily basis will catch up to you eventually. In this case, there was no significant fall or injury (at least none that my father would report or admit) that resulted in the broken hips, but rather wear and tear from the volume of medication. The doctors never questioned it, so we figured it was a reasonable cause and effect.

Broken hips are much more complicated than breaking other bones in your body, largely because your hips are involved in almost every movement you perform, from sitting to walking to standing. There almost isn't a single full-body motion you do that doesn't involve your hips, and recovery takes months to regain close to full mobility and strength. This is further complicated by the fact that it is harder to recover as you age, and having Parkinson's doesn't help since the lack of coordination and mobility makes it difficult to correctly perform a lot of the recovery exercises. As a result, my father was sent to an assisted living facility, where he was with a lot of other seniors recovering from various surgeries and injuries.

For those who are unfamiliar with an elderly care home or assisted living facility, they give you both a sense of community and isolation. On the one hand, they group you together with other people in similar and relatable situations so that you can work through hurdles and support each other. However, they also keep you away from your family members, and introverts or those who are different from the group may feel alone. My father was one of those people, as English is not his first language and Parkinson's certainly didn't help him to fit in. He needed extra assistance in almost everything he did and didn't progress as fast as others in his group. It was almost like he was the unpopular kid in school who had failing grades.

My father hated it there for obvious reasons. He was away from his usual, comfortable surroundings at home, and separated from my mother. He was also placed in a semi private room with five other people in which the only dividers were sliding curtains. The food was similar to generic cafeteria or hospital food. There was only one washroom to share between six people, and almost everyone required a nurse's assistance to use the washroom given mobility difficulties after surgery. He had a terrible time sleeping, as everyone had different sleeping schedules and tendencies, so being in a room of six people meant there were lots of lights and sounds throughout the night. There were plenty of activities, but these were mostly occupied by other members of the facility and mostly required some form of human interaction, which scared my father as he isn't very comfortable with his command of the English language.

He did try his best to get along with everyone, but wasn't able to make a deeper connection than small talk lasting a minute or so. Keep in mind that these were all folks over the age of 60, who grew up in a time in which diversity wasn't as common or celebrated, and my father was one of the only Asian people there. It also didn't help that people often fully recovered and were discharged once my father finally got to know and be comfortable with them. He was in there for two different hip rehabilitations, lasting around four months each, in the span of one year.

To counter some of these concerns and issues, we tried our best to bring him things that helped him feel more comfortable and at home. We occasionally brought him food from his favorite restaurants so that he wouldn't have to eat the cafeteria food. We also brought snacks, including some of his favorite crackers and cookies so that he would have something to help him bridge the gap in between meals.

With regards to his boredom and loneliness, he was mostly occupied during the day with the rehabilitation and recovery exercises and programs offered by the facility, but we also brought an assortment of books and his iPad to play with in his free time. Luckily, his down-time was usually filled with afternoon naps as he was exhausted from the exercise and work required to rehabilitate his hips. It was far from his usual routine of a sedentary life in front of the TV.

These months felt like years, but during this time was when I got to really see the toughness of my parents. My father continued to soldier on, like with other obstacles in his Parkinson's journey, and treated every day of rehabilitation with precision and determination. Although he was quick to update us on the bedtime routines of the people whom he shared the room with, including sleeping with a nightlight, turning on the radio for bedtime sound, facetiming loved ones at midnight, and loud snorers, he never complained to the staff or others at the care home. My father simply wanted to complete his rehab, create as little trouble as possible, and go home. The only requests he would make to the staff there would be to approve overnight leaves on weekends so that he could go home for a couple of nights. These, of course, didn't start to occur until more than halfway through his rehabilitation process.

My mother was there with him as much as she was allowed throughout this whole process. Every single day, she rushed off work at 5 pm, took public transit to get to the care home/assisted living facility, and spent the rest of the evening with my father until visitation hours ended at 9:30pm. I want to emphasize that in a span of eight months over the course of one year, my mother was at the assisted living facility every single night.

She realized this was what she had to do because it was what the family needed to pull through these trying times, and didn't complain or balk once.

Again, that is my mother. Tough as nails.

I would occasionally visit about twice a week, and did my best to keep the house in order without both of my parents there, as I lived at home during this time.

Do I have regrets about not going frequently enough to visit my dad looking back on it? Yes, but I was working lots of overtime hours at KPMG and going through the CA education process, and my parents were adamant that my studies came first.

Classic stereotypical Asian parenting.

It provided the perfect cover-up for another reason I didn't go as often; it pained me so much to see the condition that my father would be in some days when I went to visit. It's tough to see someone you love in that position, and knowing there is nothing you can do to fix it.

I would do my best to hold it together on the drive home with my mother, and then proceed to cry myself to sleep almost every time. I didn't want to put myself through that every day, and it was selfish of me to not visit as often.

I simply wasn't tough enough.

Having learned all this about toughness through my father's journey with Parkinson's, I've come to understand that toughness involves an element of vulnerability. It isn't about being macho or never expressing pain; we are unable to exemplify toughness or the ability to persevere through difficult situations if we don't first encounter hardship. In fact, most of us don't even fully comprehend how strong we are until we are put into a position in which we have no choice.

After all, how tough can you really become if everything is sunshine, lollipops, and handed to you on a silver platter?

There are endless examples of ordinary people demonstrating feats of superhuman strength in life or death situations, and toughness works the exact same way. It is not a sign of weakness to show vulnerability; rather, it is only an opportunity to see how tough we are capable of being. Learning to be vulnerable leads to tremendous personal growth, helping you to develop strength, compassion, and respect, which will in turn lead to overcoming your fear and demons.

Understanding this has given me the toughness to be comfortable enough to share my story with anyone willing to listen.

My family's journey has also taught me that toughness comes in all shapes and sizes, and often isn't defined by anything physical. I've learned that toughness is a mentality, and that most of my life's problems are really trivial and miniscule when we put them into the proper perspective.

After all, what right do I have to complain about anything that happens in my day-to-day life if my parents don't complain about their circumstances?

Is it actually that big of a deal that the service at the restaurant was a little slow? Or that the lady in the car in front of me was driving so slowly that I missed the green light?

I was getting upset and complaining about the most meaningless things when I put it all into perspective. There will always be someone on earth willing to trade places with me, and I need to remember that when I'm in situations where I feel as though I'm getting the short end of the straw. We are all blessed beyond belief.

Letting these minor inconveniences dictate my emotions and actions is definitely the opposite of toughness. It's downright petty, childish, and immature.

The best part in all of this is that we all have the ability to change the way we view things. It can start this second, and there is no shortage of opportunities for practice. Toughness is about not being rattled or affected by anything that happens to us, and having the discipline to avoid distractions. In the case of those affected by illness and disease, it's about accepting fear and continuing to persevere through the next wave of obstacles. This understanding of toughness has changed my perspective, and helped me to focus my time and energy on what truly matters in my life:

Family. Friends. Legacy. Charitable causes.

If it doesn't fit into one of your buckets, it is simply not worth the time or emotional drain. Develop the mental toughness to look past it and not let it distract you from your big picture.

Take a few minutes to ponder instances in which toughness has been evident in your story. How can you take that mentality and use it to change other aspects of your life for the better?

Chapter 10: Sadness

The next life lesson/concept is by far the hardest one for me to write about. This chapter almost took the same amount of time to write as the other seven concepts combined. The reason was because of all the emotions that this chapter brought out of me, and the tears shed while writing. It is the most present and lingering out of the seven, and definitely one that you initially reject at first, until you slowly understand its role within illness/disease and life in general. I know personally it's taken a long time for me to accept and embrace this, and I'm well aware that it's going to be something I will need to constantly work on for the rest of my life.

This is the concept of sadness.

Sadness come in many shapes and sizes, and is often described using other words such as disappointment, depression, gloom, heartbreak, etc. It's hard to define sadness, and the best thing I can come up with is to say it is the opposite of happiness.

Instead of trying to offer my own deeper interpretation and meaning of the concept, I'll just go right to the Merriam-Webster's definition:

"Causing or associated with grief or unhappiness." [11]

Even the world's most popular dictionary is unsure how to describe sadness other than by comparing it to happiness.

Those with families affected by disease/illness can tell you there is definitely no shortage of sad or disappointing moments. For me, a couple memories instantly come to mind with regards to my father, and there aren't many days that go by in which I don't think of these instances at least once.

One of them takes place in an all too familiar location - the pre-operation patient waiting area. For those who are fortunate enough not to know, it is the area in which patients are screened and given all of their pre-surgery information, medication, and other treatments before entering the operation room. My mother and I were there with my father waiting before he was about to have the battery in his chest replaced. It was a simple procedure that every individual implanted with the DBS machine is required to do every 3-4 years, as that is the battery life of the machine. As we sat there and waited for my father's turn to go into the operation room, a nurse came by to perform all of the pre-surgery protocol, including the standard questionnaire, blood pressure test, and IV.

The questionnaire started with a few simple awareness

questions such as "What is your name?" and "What are you here for?". These questions were basic, didn't involve much thinking, and my father crushed through them as if it were a race.

Then came a question that I think about every single day... "Do you ever get depressed or feel sad?".

It seemed like time had stopped the moment the nurse asked the question. I was completely taken aback by it, as it hit me out of the blue. She had tossed five or six underhand lobs over the plate and then all of a sudden unexpectedly threw a 100-mph fastball. I definitely didn't have time to prepare for the answer to come; in fact, I wasn't even completely sure that I ever wanted to know the answer to that question. However, I was in the room and there was no way for me to escape before the response came.

For the rest of my life, I will always remember the answer to that question and the interaction that followed between my father and the nurse:

Nurse: "Do you ever get depressed or feel sad?"

My father: "Yes."

Nurse, clearly understanding the weight of the answer: "Of course. It's only normal to feel depressed or sad occasionally given the circumstances. It would raise a red flag if you never got depressed!"

Uncomfortable laughter from everyone in the room

I almost instantly broke down after my father had answered, trying my hardest to put on a straight face and hold back tears. But the nurse was right; it would have actually been more perplexing if my father had answered the question with a no. If I had given the full scenario to any stranger, it would make logical sense to assume that almost every single person would predict the answer to that question to be yes.

Yet, here I was completely shocked by the answer and balling my eyes out in front of my parents and the nurse, who all reacted as if nothing had happened. It was at that moment I realized that even though my parents had been able to shield me from these situations throughout the journey, it didn't mean that they never happened.

Ignorance can be bliss, and I was definitely ignorant to the fact that my parents had gone through hundreds of these situations and feelings over the course of 15+ years since my father was initially diagnosed.

Actually, they had gone through so many of those emotional scenarios with thousands of tears already shed that they no longer even reacted to them - I was just much further behind in the process, and purposely by my parents' design. It seems silly looking back that I never considered the emotions and thoughts that must have gone through my father's head all those years as Parkinson's progressed and started to take over his body. As I alluded to in the chapter on toughness, it takes weakness to see just how strong we really are. The mental toughness my father exudes in living through all these recurring negative thoughts and still being able to find joy in everyday life is something that makes him one of my heroes.

While it was one of the saddest moments of my life to date, we have never discussed it as a family. I don't think I'll ever be ready for that conversation, and nothing more needs to be said or explained.

Another example in which sadness is clearly present in my father's journey with Parkinson's isn't a specific moment or incident, but rather something that happens on a regular basis; it is the looks and stares he receives when he is out in public. As you are aware by now being this far into the book, Parkinson's disease causes unnatural physical movements and restrictions that look different to the average person. It doesn't help that Parkinson's provides no physical signs that an individual is disabled, causing a lot of staring from curious strangers.

There are no oddly shaped body parts or wounds. Let's face it, as humans we have an attraction to events and things we see that are unusual, whether they be car crashes, violence, grotesque injuries, blood, or shiny/bright colours. We simply cannot turn away from them. As a result, my father receives a lot of intriguing looks from strangers when he is out in public.

Some of the more noticeable situations include activities or scenarios in which my father is in the same place for an extended period of time and there isn't much else going on. These range anywhere from standing in an elevator to eating at a restaurant. The looks come from people who have no ill-will or bad intent, but are rather just curious and bored. There are also a lot of people who quickly identify that something is different about my father, and choose to spare him the awkwardness by not looking.

However, children are on the complete opposite spectrum of that, as they don't know any better and are often the most curious. In the initial years of my father being diagnosed, he was extremely self-conscious and aware of the eyes that would stare at him in public settings, and frequently resorted to looking at the ground. After all, it was the only place he could glance in which he would be sure that no one was staring back at him. It was terribly uncomfortable for my father, and it took a long time for him to confidently look up without care. I think it is still something my father works on every time we are in public, and will be something he continues to fight from a mental standpoint for the rest of his life. The majority of us try our hardest to fit into society, and don't necessarily want any unrequested attention. Having people constantly stare at you because you look different definitely hurts your self-esteem, and brings a lot of sadness.

Most people spend their whole lives doing everything they can to avoid these negative feelings, oftentimes sacrificing long term happiness and goals in order to create short-term ecstasy so as not to have to experience sadness. Almost all of us are guilty of succumbing to retail therapy, happy hour drinks, or a tub of ice cream when something stresses us out or doesn't go our way. All of these reactions are designed to create temporary feelings of relief and happiness, and delay our ability to feel disappointment or sadness. However, they are not real, and force us to suppress these emotions.

As the famous author Mark Manson writes: "The desire for more positive experience is itself a negative experience. And, paradoxically, the acceptance of one's negative experience is itself a positive experience." [12]

I've learned throughout this journey since my father's diagnosis that you can only suppress sadness for so long, and that it is one of the most important emotions to be felt. As I mature, I realize that sadness and negative emotions/events are just as important in our journey through life as the happy times. In fact, we often learn our most crucial life lessons in times of disappointment and sorrow.

It was actually through sport that I had this revelation. There are countless quotes from coaches/athletes who tell you that teams learn more from losses than victories, and that winning often covers up glaring weaknesses and places for improvement, both of which are important to identify for future success. It is important for teams to experience losing so that they can sharpen their focus and become battle-tested. The same holds true for our lives. I had managed to put the two and two together, and it made perfect sense.

I was sold.

The next step in the process after understanding the importance of sadness was to comprehend why it was in my human nature to avoid such emotions and experiences at almost virtually any cost. I knew it wouldn't be as simple as flipping a switch to start embracing sad moments. As I explained to you in the chapter on toughness, I was often a coward when it came to those moments and did my best to avoid them.

Heck, I couldn't even tell people my father had Parkinson's because I was too afraid of the sadness and pity that moment would entail.

I am very disappointed in myself for this. We are a family, and we should be tackling these things together. It was selfish of me and I definitely wasn't pulling my weight.

I started to perform a self-assessment and concluded that the biggest reason was because the emotion of sadness is uncomfortable, and is often the result of undesired situations/scenarios. As humans, we tend to resort to decisions that keep us in our own little safe space, hardly ever venturing outside of our comfort zone. This subconscious strategy is based on our survival instincts. The theory makes perfect sense - if we only do things we know are safe and comfortable, the chances of our survival increase.

Doing things outside of our comfort zone often creates the feeling of unfamiliarity, which is tied to danger and a decrease in our chances of survival. This concept is even repeatedly portrayed and over-emphasized in pop culture. In horror movies, the characters never die in a place they frequently encounter and are familiar with. They usually find themselves in danger when they decide to go on a trip out of town or venture into the wilderness or even lesser used places of their house like the attic. The same can be said for fashion; we tend to ridicule new fashion trends and unique outfits because they are unfamiliar to us and our initial defense mechanism is to dismiss them.

However, as we see people adopting the trends and the resulting outfits become more familiar to us, we begin to accept them. Take the trends of flashier colours and tighter fits for example - oftentimes, we end up embracing them so much that we end up purchasing the clothing for ourselves. Understanding that we subconsciously default to the comfortable path was important for me, as I just now needed to identify these situations in the moment, and consciously make the decision to take the opposite road. Instead of avoiding sadness and grief, I needed to face these moments head on and embrace the life lessons waiting for me.

Another barrier to this is that, as a male, there is a stigma to showing emotions that may be portrayed as vulnerable. It is often seen as weakness and something that is undesired or just not what "real men" do, whatever that phrase even means. Historically, men have always been viewed to be the strength and breadwinner of the family, and a "manly" image usually resembled something along the lines of rugged, independent, tough, burly, and dominant. Vulnerability and the need to reach out for help definitely didn't equate to the societal image of men, and as a result, it was often hidden and concealed.

After all, signs of weakness are not embraced under Darwinism and natural selection.

Although the stigma has evolved throughout the years

with many male celebrities publicly embracing their vulnerabilities associated with mental health and depression, we still have a long way to go as a society. As an only child growing up, I felt the need and responsibility to be the "man of the house" given my father's situation, which held me back from embracing my sadness as I didn't want to seem vulnerable in front of my parents. In a way, I still struggle with this today but for a much different reason. I'm afraid that my parents will see me feeling sad and attribute the blame to themselves, when in reality it is really nobody's fault. I've yet to find a solution to this, but continue to search for the answer.

As I've highlighted throughout the book and will continue to do, dealing with bad breaks in life isn't something that you figure out the solution to and never have to think about again. You must work on it every single day as the pain never goes away; you just get stronger and find better ways to handle it.

I also needed to understand that my current approach wasn't working. Although I was often able to make decisions that would allow me to avoid situations of sadness and grief, I found that the feelings never fully disappeared, but were instead only suppressed. These negative emotions would bundle up every time they were pushed down and not allowed to surface, until eventually they could no longer be held in, leading to outbursts that I made sure only happened when I was alone. I can't even estimate the number of times growing up that I cried alone in the shower or in bed.

It is an important exercise to take a step back, assess our current responses to certain situations, understand our human nature's subconscious response, and determine whether it is truly the best approach to take. We don't live a meaningful and fulfilled life by constantly avoiding our problems and neglecting everything that is outside of our comfort zone.

This journey has taught me that sadness should be fully experienced, as much as we crave and savour happiness. I cried a lot growing up and still do to this day; after all, no matter how mentally strong we are, these situations aren't easy to deal with. I've also learned that showing vulnerability is one of the strongest things you can do. There is no strength or honor in hiding weakness and emotions, and suppressing it while it slowly eats at you on the inside. It takes a tough person to openly acknowledge that things aren't okay and that you need support.

The first step to overcoming any obstacle or barrier is acknowledging it exists in the first place.

Most people have that issue - heck, I had that problem for the first 15 years of my father's diagnosis. The second I let vulnerability and sadness into my life, everything changed for the better. It's funny how that works - the more I tried to be happy, the sadder I was; yet the more I embraced sadness, the happier I became.

I recently came across a quote that changed my perspective on sadness even more, and will hopefully help you to embrace it with open arms:

"In the course of your lives, without any plan on your part, you'll come to see suffering that will break your heart. When it happens, and it will, don't turn away from it; turn towards it. That is the moment when change is born." – Melinda Gates[13]

First off, how beautiful and eloquent is that quote? It simply couldn't have been better said. In fact, if you think about it, this is actually what I've been subconsciously trying to do for the past 3 years since publicly sharing my father's story.

Secondly, this was the missing piece to my self-analysis. Sure, it was important to experience sadness because without understanding it completely, how are we to appreciate happiness and the opposite side of the spectrum? You don't appreciate the sun as much if it doesn't rain every once in a while.

However, this helped me understand a deeper reason as to why sadness should be embraced and was not something to run or hide from. It brought clarity to my big picture, and a purpose to all of this confusion over the last 15+ years.

I needed to fully experience the sadness and let it motivate me enough not to sit idle on the sidelines anymore, to have it hurt so much that I'd start telling people about my father's story, and then actively attempt to raise funds and awareness for Parkinson's disease in the hopes of helping others who are in similar situations. To repeatedly keep drawing on the well of heartbreak so that I continue to push through barriers and obstacles that would make any individual without a purpose give up.

After all, anyone who has a "why" can conquer any "how".

This is exactly what is happening in my life right now. The process of accepting sadness and disappointment definitely isn't easy and has taken a lot of work, but it's been necessary. It's even motivated me to write the book that you are currently reading, all in the name of trying to raise funds and awareness, as well as getting others to positively act on their misfortunes! I am embarrassed to say that this process started a lot later than I'm proud of, but better late than never - never would have been one of my biggest regrets. If you're in a similar situation, please don't let it be one of yours.

Learn to understand and embrace every emotion, both positive and negative, that you feel on a daily basis. They all have something to teach us.

Trust me, it's worth it.

Take a few minutes to ponder instances in which you've repressed negative emotions - why, and how you can react to those situations moving forward? What lessons can you learn from them.

Chapter 11: Love

This chapter is more dedicated to my mother than it is my father, and her part in this whole journey. She definitely deserves it; as you may know, illness/disease doesn't just affect a single individual. It impacts everyone within its radius, and requires us all to play a part.

The concept is love.

Love is a funny word. It is an all-encompassing term that we use to describe almost any positive situation and emotion, especially in trying times. To some, it means intimacy, desire, commitment, and attraction. To others, it means sacrifice, pain, unity, heartbreak, passion, or even happiness. There are so many definitions of the word "love" that I'm sure if you asked five different people randomly, you would get five different explanations.

To me, love has changed its meaning many times as I've continued through this journey through life.

When I was a child, love meant family and physical possessions. Due to my limited exposure to the real world and all of the possibilities and problems that it presents, life was simple. I learned to love my family and my toys. Those were the only things that I interacted with on a daily basis.

During my teenage and adolescent years, love meant physical attraction and desire. At that age, it's about relationships with other teenagers and adolescents, and being physically intimate.

As I continue to journey through life, love to me currently means sacrifice, unselfishness, support, dedication, and teamwork.

Our definitions of love change on a continuous basis depending on our personal experiences and the people we surround ourselves with. Love can be associated with an object, a person, an idea, or even an abstract concept. It can be both a friend and an enemy, and is regularly found in the least suspected places.

Merriam-Webster's definition of love is the following:

(1): strong affection for another arising out of kinship or personal ties[14]

(2): attraction based on sexual desire[14]

(3): affection based on admiration, benevolence, or common interests[14]

As you see, it is hard for even the world's best

dictionaries to pinpoint exactly what this four-letter word means.

In the drafting of this book, I kept delaying the writing of this chapter as I was scared of the emotional toll it would take on me. It is a lot to think about my parents' love for each other and the sacrifices that my mother has had to make as a result of this disease. A large part of my personal definition of love is due to her influence, and seeing all that she has done to take care of my father and be by his side every step of the way. She is truly the rock of our family.

I don't even know where to start in explaining the presence and effect that love has when someone in your family is diagnosed with an illness/disease. It is the security blanket we fall back on to ensure us that everything will be ok, and that we don't have to go through these things alone, akin to Linus' blue blanket! Love is present in all acts of caregiving. For my parents' journey, it started on their wedding day when they said their vows and proclaimed "I do." If you are unfamiliar with the traditional wedding vows, they go something like this:

"I, (Name), take you, (Name), to be my wife (or husband), to have and to hold from this day forward, for better, for worse, for richer, for poorer, in sickness and in health, to love and to cherish, till death us do part, in the presence of God I make this vow."

My parents, both being born Catholic, were married in a church and recited vows identical to these. This was the beginning of their promise to love each other for the rest of their lives regardless of the circumstances. As you'll notice reading the vows, they pertain to both extremes, and a commitment to approaching the thick and thin together.

I'd imagine a significant number of couples proclaim these vows tongue in cheek, and simply include them in their wedding ceremony because it has been a tradition historically. After all, the divorce rate is roughly 50%, so there's plenty of reason to believe at least one partner in the marriage didn't take them to heart. Then again, no one has a crystal ball to see what the future holds and people change drastically over the years.

My mother proved to be the complete opposite and continues to exemplify the definition of marriage on a daily basis, especially regarding the phrase "in sickness and in health".

Skipping ahead 15 years after they got married to when my father was diagnosed with Parkinson's, I can only imagine what went through my mother's mind when the doctor told them the news. As I've never actually discussed that moment with my parents and don't have much context, I often replay the day in my head and wonder what went through their minds. I was 12 years old, so I actually don't have any recollection of the day in general. I think throughout the course of the book, I've provided little sprinkles here and there for you to picture what my father was probably thinking, like the fact that he was depressed for a short period of time after the initial diagnosis. But then again, can you really blame him?

As for the thoughts that went through my mother's head, this is where I start to marvel at her love and commitment. Most of us desire to be in relationships for companionship - sure, physical attraction is great, but as the years progress, it is something that slowly fades away. As a result, most successful marriages are the result of strong friendships and a joy in doing things together. It's hard to live with someone you have nothing in common with. When I think about myself 30 years from now, I imagine being retired with my wife and spending our days gardening, playing board games, volunteering, doing leisurely activities, and traveling the world.

Almost all of these things were taken away from my mother when my father was diagnosed with Parkinson's. That is not to say they are impossible, but in the majority of cases including theirs, a disease such as Parkinson's will cause significant financial and emotional stress in the family. It's definitely difficult to do a lot of physical activities together with Parkinson's. I can only imagine my mother thinking about the future at the time of my father's diagnosis and being devastated. Instead of traveling the world, she will have to work years beyond her retirement age to help with the financial burden and lack of savings as my father has been unable to work.

On top of that, my mother will have to continue to take on an increasing amount of duties around the house and act more like a caregiver as my father's condition worsens. This includes cleaning the house, cooking meals, doing laundry, and everything else that a person living by themselves would be responsible for, except double the amount.

It is certainly a tall order as my mother continues to age.

Companionship will also continue to suffer as the effects of Parkinson's take its toll on my father's ability to speak and communicate. I've tried my best to help whenever I can, but it's tough when I'm not there every day as we don't live together anymore.

My mother has never complained about having to take care of my father or the predicament that she is in because of the wedding vows she took and the love they share, but I can't imagine how hard it must have been to say goodbye to any plans that they had for life into their sunset years. My father has become a shell of the man she said "I do" to on their wedding day, yet her commitment has not wavered even one bit.

I don't think I would have been upset if she decided this was not what she signed up for and left; a lot of people have done so in situations like this or less. After all, we all only have one life to fulfill our hopes and ambitions. I wish I could give her the world for the sacrifices she makes on a daily basis - she truly deserves it and more.

But that's just not how it works sometimes. No matter how much positivity you choose to approach life with, sometimes it can truly feel unfair.

However, she wouldn't have it any other way. If she did, she wouldn't still be here. Love conquers all.

One of the most vivid images I have to describe love is when I would accompany my mother on visits to the hospital or care home where my father was and it was time to head home for the night. My mother would make sure everything my father needed for the rest of the night (including snacks, iPad, phone charger, medication, water, etc.) was organized and all within reach for him.

They would then hold hands, hug, and my mother would look my father in the eyes and tell him that she loved him, everything would be alright, and that he could call her anytime. She could sense the fear within him, having to spend another night by himself in a place that was uncomfortable and unfamiliar. It also didn't help that he had trouble communicating as English is his second language. This was followed by a big kiss and silence as we walked out of the building and back to our car.

I was literally witnessing true love; my mother would be on the verge of tears, but somehow always held it together. She was just as fearful, yet always showed a face that convinced you that for some reason she knew things would really be alright. After 30+ years of marriage, the love they share is still just as passionate. The thought of not being able to be there with my father through tough times made my mother miserable, especially given the circumstances.

This exact goodbye has happened over 200 times throughout this journey so far, which is about 200 times too many if you ask me.

The second I realized what true love looked like, I made a pact with myself in my early 20s to never get married until I found someone who would love me as much as my mother loves my father, and vice versa. Finding that type of relationship and commitment is definitely worth having your heart broken a million times, to the point where you want to quit searching ever again and convince yourself there isn't anyone out there for you. Do whatever you can to find it, and when you do (oh, you will inevitably regardless of how dire your current situation feels), never take it for granted. It will be one of the most meaningful things you do in life. That's the biggest lesson about love I've learned from my parents throughout this journey.

In Chelsey Ann Bogaczewicz, I have found it. My heart couldn't be more full.

Another aspect of love that my mother exemplifies so well is being present. In this day and age, there are many reasons and excuses that we often come up with not to be present. Our lives only speed up as we get older and there are a lot of distractions/temptations that attract our attention. Sometimes, even when we are physically present, our attention is divided amongst cell phones or other devices that take our focus away.

Despite not owning a car and solely relying on public transit, my mother has never missed a doctor's appointment or any other event that has been associated with my father's health. Usually, these matters don't happen outside of work hours (9-5 Monday to Friday), but my mom has never hesitated to take the day off, put in a couple of overtime hours, switch shifts, work on a weekend, or start work earlier. She has done whatever it takes to be right next to my father at every appointment he's had, because she doesn't want him to have to go through it alone. Not to mention the hospital stays and care home rehabilitation cycles that I touched on earlier in the chapter about toughness.

My father always showed a tough exterior look but my mother knew that he was terrified on the inside, and needed support through those trying times. It definitely didn't help that he lacked confidence with the English language either, so she was also his translator to doctors and nurses.

Over the years, she has never failed to sacrifice her own personal, social, and leisure time to be right by my father's side. It has significantly affected her ability to pursue any purposeful or time-consuming hobbies, as well as the capability to make many meaningful friends, but it is a sacrifice that she has never hesitated to make and continues to do so on a regular basis.

At the same time, she used any left-over energy and time to make sure she was providing me with ample love and attention. I have no idea how she did and continues to do it. My mother prided herself on being the hardest worker in the room and never leaving work until everything was done, then coming home and having to cook dinner before taking care of my father and making sure I had completed all of my homework. I feel pathetic when I say that I often go to sleep before 10 pm after a hard day's work. Moms are truly a different breed.

My mother has taught me so much about love throughout this journey, without us ever having a formal discussion about it. But that's the way we were as a family and how I was parented. It mostly consisted of teaching by example, and required me to be extremely self-aware. She also taught me that love isn't always rainbows and lollipops, and that it can be filled with heartbreak and sadness, especially when someone you love is in pain and there is nothing you can do to fix it. Sometimes, it just downright sucks, but nevertheless, love is always worth it.

For better, for worse, for richer, for poorer, in sickness and in health. It hasn't always been smooth sailing between my parents and they certainly didn't sign up for this twisted turn of events when they got married, but love prevails every time.

Every. Single. Time.

Love will always be evident in these circumstances because a disease or illness affects more than just the person diagnosed. It can come from a significant other, family member, child, friend, online community, support groups, etc. My family's story isn't unique or special.

Nobody ever fights alone.

You just have to be looking for it.

Take a few minutes to ponder how love is evident in your story, and what you can do to show more love to others in similar situations.

Chapter 12: The Meaning of Life

The last and most critical concept is one that isn't understood as quickly as the others that have been previously described. This one involves seeing the bigger picture, and combining all those moments and memories from prior chapters in an attempt to make sense of it all. It is the overarching lesson and the most meaningful thing I have learned throughout this journey with my father and Parkinson's disease. This is the concept I have held onto in an attempt to give meaning and purpose to the set of cards my family has been dealt.

The seventh concept is the meaning of life.

It is by far the most personal of the seven, and one that doesn't have incorrect definitions. Just like love, if you asked ten strangers to define the meaning of life, you would receive a different answer from everybody, some which you never even considered to be possible answers. After all, most people spend their whole lives in search of this answer, and aren't convinced that they ever figure it out. Some even stop wondering.

Parkinson's disease has helped to clarify my own interpretation of the meaning of life, and to see the bigger picture of our existence. But first, before I provide my definition, let us see what the dictionary says. Oh wait - Merriam-Webster does not have a definition because it is a phrase rather than words. The dictionary has definitions for the words "meaning" and "life", but they have a significantly different explanation than the sum of its parts. As a result, we don't actually have a starting point in defining the phrase!

My interpretation of the meaning of life has come from a combination of things, from reading about others' perspectives to personal time spent reflecting. It has also broadened and changed over time as I continue to go through the wonderful journey we call life. These are obviously my own interpretations and may not align with what you have figured to be the meaning of life so far. However, it doesn't mean that either one of us is wrong - after all, our responses are largely influenced by our circumstances and experiences. Through my family's story, I've narrowed it down to three principles:

1. Giving
2. Legacy
3. Triumph over difficulty or hardship

Let's take a deep dive on each one of these principles individually.

Giving:

This is the easiest concept out of the three to relate to, as it is one of the most common principles shared. We often strive to achieve this magically abstract idea known as happiness, but never understand where it exists and how we can produce more of it. However, one of the most agreed upon methods is to help others, and more specifically those who are less fortunate than us. Happiness generally lies in giving without expectations or personal gain.

It's actually an interesting concept when you think about it.

We've been trained our whole lives to do whatever it takes to accumulate physical possessions, often sacrificing things such as health and time for money. Even as children, we are frequently jealous of others' toys and games. Yet, it's commonly known that giving without the prospect of receiving is the most surefire way to create happiness.

Oh, the irony!

The next logical question from this train of thought is whether it matters who we choose to give to, and how we do so?

As human beings, we yearn for connection and community. In fact, it's so important to our survival that it has its own level on Maslow's hierarchy of needs, known as love and belonging. This level on the pyramid is defined by the need for intimate relationships, human interaction, and belonging to a community. It's also been a trend that has evolved throughout humankind, from tribes, to cities, to the present day with online social media groups and message boards. We find community in the least expected places, including sports team fan bases and video games.

However, humans are more complicated than that - it isn't okay to just be part of a community, but it has to provide us with meaningful belonging. We feel inclusion only if we are offering value or the community is providing value to us. Once we are in a meaningful community that fits all of the criteria, we often stop short of nothing to protect and grow the community.

As a result, we tend to create bonds with other members, share our knowledge and resources, offer support, and try to constantly improve the community in any way, shape, or form, so that we can look upon it with pride and happiness. In a way, it almost justifies the fights that often occur as a result of sporting events!

Throughout my family's journey, I've come to this epiphany and how the concepts of giving and community perfectly mesh with Parkinson's disease.

This is an opportunity to help and inspire others, while directly benefiting my father and his situation as well. Raising funds and awareness for Parkinson's has brought me more joy than anything else I've ever done or accomplished in my life, and it isn't even close.

I've also discovered this little community known as the planet Earth and the human species. It's been surreal and emotional at times to see the amount of support we've received when talking about the disease or when my father has been struggling.

A funny thing about communities is that all members are able to relate to each other to a certain extent through shared interests, experiences, or other commonalities that make them a member of that community in the first place. Personally, I can't think of a bigger community than humanity.

As human beings, we are all able to relate regardless of language, gender, religion, race, wealth, etc. It doesn't matter where you were born or your life experiences to date, it's not hard to identify other humans who are more vulnerable than we are and in need of support, we all have that soft spot in our hearts.

The community of people who I have bonded with on my personal journey has been instrumental in the healing process. Knowing what it feels like on the receiving end and how that has changed my life motivates me every single day to pay it forward. I don't think I would have shared my story without their support. Give without expectation, and you end up receiving tenfold. Funny how that works.

Parkinson's has helped me realize that one of the meanings of life is to give and help those who are less fortunate, which in turn makes the world a better place for all. We all strive to better the human tribe, and all those who belong to our community.

Legacy:

The second of the three meanings of life that I have is the concept of legacy. As humans, we have always craved the idea of status or the feeling of being important. This ties back to the previously mentioned concept of yearning to be a part of a meaningful community.

At its foundation, a community that evolves over the course of time tends to shed its weakest members only to be replaced by new members who provide more value. Simple real-world examples of this would include employees being fired at work and being replaced by new hires, as well as sports teams making cuts and looking to acquire new players. Our ability to make a positive and significant contribution to the world improves our chances of staying a member within that tribe, which in turn improves our chances of survival.

After all, companies don't often fire their top salesman and sports teams rarely trade away their star players.

Our need for status and attention is evident in almost

everything we do, from picking physical fights with others in order to exert dominance to lying, cheating, and stealing just to win a board game. It explains why we boast and celebrate our accomplishments and awards. In the current age, that has translated to doing whatever it takes to gain more followers and likes on social media platforms. An obsession for attention and status is currently at an all-time high.

The irony lies in the fact that we only live for about 75-80 years (if we're lucky), and humanity has existed for anywhere from 5,000 to 6,000,000 years depending on where you fall on the science vs religion debate, with no end in the foreseeable future. This means our existence is miniscule in the timeline of humanity. In order for our importance and status to survive into future generations, we need to create a legacy that spans longer than our lifetime. The goal isn't to live forever, it's to create something that does.

When we think of legacy, we often refer to successful people who have either created businesses, set athletic records, or invented something. People such as Steve Jobs, Thomas Edison, Michael Jordan, Jeff Bezos, Wayne Gretzky and Bill Gates instantly come to mind.

However, the majority of the population has not achieved anything that has garnered worldwide attention and notoriety to that degree. In those cases, their legacy often involves an element that never comes to mind in these types of conversations... their children!

As sons and daughters, we were raised and molded into the people we are today by our parents. The values and morals that we hold and trust to make important decisions come mostly as a result of what our parents have taught us. As children, if we are poorly behaved or do something bad, others perceive and judge it as the result of bad parenting. When our parents pass away, their worldly possessions are passed down for us to enjoy and build upon to give to future generations. Family legacies are also travel down from generation to generation through surnames, which has created a historic desire for male offspring.

We are an extension of our parents to the future generation, and who we end up being often becomes a part of their legacy.

This adds an interesting twist in my quest to find both the meaning of my father's diagnosis and the meaning of life. My father may have had the ability to mold his own legacy cut short and limited by factors that were outside of his control, but at the same time, both he and my mother spent a great deal of time, effort, and money to raise me right and put me in the position I am in today.

As I stated in my story, they even moved halfway across the world for me!

I am their legacy, and what I do from now on continues to affect it. I owe everything I have and everything I am to my parents. Realizing this has affected my behavior tremendously, as legacies are both positive and negative. After all, Hitler left behind a legacy that still has a lasting impact to this day, but it definitely cannot be seen as positive. I've tried to be more of a positively contributing member to society by volunteering in the community, spending more time with my parents, being more conscious of my environmental footprint, donating to charitable causes, and being a hard-working employee.

Hopefully these are all things that my parents can be proud of and will add to their legacy. In addition, this discovery has created a thought-provoking connection. As I continue to raise funds and awareness for Parkinson's Disease (including through this book!), because I am the legacy of my parents, would that not make my father's legacy the fact that he helped to make the lives of those affected by Parkinson's better?

This in turn motivates me to push as hard as I can to share our story, which will only continue to expand his legacy left behind.

Perhaps I'm irrationally making this all up, and forcing an argument that has no merit in order to justify the hand I've been dealt. Either way, it has helped me put things into perspective and motivated me to make a positive contribution to society in an attempt to help those who are less fortunate.

If that's the result of a made-up story, I think I'm ok with that.

The goal isn't to live forever, it's to create a positive legacy that has the potential to do so.

If you pick up nothing else from this book, I hope you're able to adopt this mindset/concept. It has helped me turn an unfortunate break into the biggest blessing of my life.

Triumph Over Difficulty/Hardship:

The majority of people would accept a statement in which the hypothesis for the meaning of life was some type of pursuit of happiness, which I alluded to as a by-product of helping others in the first concept. It seems almost common sense to think that - after all, who doesn't want to be happy? Most of the things we desire in life, whether they are objects or experiences, we only crave because we feel they would make us happy or joyful.

However, this hedonistic thinking is a very dangerous mindset and one that can lead to your life spiraling out of control. Let me explain.

Happiness is a funny concept. Everyone has a different theory as to how to create it, yet no one has a certain method. At times, it's even hard to define exactly what the word means and how we know we've achieved it. It regularly shows up as a surprise and in the most unexpected ways. Sometimes, intentionally pursuing it pushes it further away. The threshold is different for every individual on earth, and changes as we become used to our surroundings. Doing most things repeatedly generally creates less happiness as we do them more frequently. As I write this and think about the concept of happiness, I'm not even sure I can define what it means to me and the threshold at which I would be satisfied to say that I am happy.

The most important thing to understand is that happiness is not a constant, nor a guarantee in life. Every individual human being will experience a different degree and frequency of happiness over the course of their lives. Some people get lucky with the cards they've been dealt and have more opportunities to experience happiness than others. Generally speaking, an individual who is born healthy in a first world country to two parents will have higher odds to achieve more happiness throughout their lifetime than an individual who is born in a war-torn country with a disability and separated from their parents.

However, what you choose to do with the hand you're dealt is obviously up to you and some people don't take full advantage of their opportunities.

How are we supposed to pursue something we're not entirely sure how to create or even if it will ever be present due to circumstances outside of our control? Would this then not inevitably set us up for guaranteed disappointment and failure?

As a result, my argument is that it's a false prophecy to claim that life should be about the pursuit of happiness. This is why I haven't made happiness one of the meanings of life, even though I alluded to it in the section on giving above. That would be potentially leading people into a ditch they can't dig their way out of. Instead, we should be defining our life around values and concepts that are constants in our lives, and guaranteed to be experienced regardless of your religion, birthplace, race, gender, etc.

There is literally only one that comes to mind, and that is the concept of difficulty/suffering - or simply put, pain. It is a constant that everyone at some point will experience, regardless of how fortunate you are. After all, you will inevitably outlive some of your loved ones if you are to have a long and prosperous life. Given the negative connotations of this concept and our life's quest to make everything positive, the meaning of life should be character development through hardship, and being strong enough to fight through pain to make something positive out of it.

One of my favorite quotes to sum this concept up comes from a book called Everything is F*cked: A Book About Hope by Mark Manson:

"Because pain is the universal constant of life, the opportunities to grow from that pain are constant in life. All that is required is that we don't numb it, that we don't look away. All that is required is that we engage it and find the value and meaning in it." [16]

This is simplistic in nature, yet hard to implement. Much like I explained in the chapter on sadness, we all have a tendency to run away from pain or negative emotions. After all, it puts us outside of our comfort zones, where our bodies subconsciously crave for us to stay within as it increases our chance of survival. However, we also lose out on the opportunities for personal growth and the lessons to be learned.

Running away from pain so that we don't feel the negative emotions associated with it isn't a solution. We've already discussed that pain is a constant in life and inevitably everyone comes across it. You can only run for so long. While you are avoiding pain with short-term pleasures such shopping sprees, alcohol, gambling, food, vacations, you unknowingly dig yourself deeper and deeper into the hole, making it more and more difficult to face. Pain is nature's way of telling us that something needs to change or it's time for us to grow, so don't ignore the signs.

The meaning of life shouldn't be the pursuit of happiness, but rather the complete opposite. It should be continuous character growth through hardship in order to increase the threshold of our own pain tolerance, so that we don't experience as many negative emotions when going through these situations in the future. The goal should be to become the best versions of ourselves, and to be so content with our constant effort in doing so that we are better able to accept unfortunate events that are outside of our control, because there is really nothing we could have done to prevent it.

Of course, we often learn more during times of defeat than the joys of victory. It isn't necessarily happiness that fulfills us, but rather the tolerance of hardship and sorrow.

Ironically enough, happiness requires the experience of pain to develop.

Now that I've explained the three different meanings of life, what does it all mean in the grand scheme of things?

I can't speak on your behalf because I don't know your life journey and story. For me, this has played a significant role in trying to place meaning and understanding to my father's diagnosis. While I still don't know why it happened in this form to my family, pain and suffering are unavoidable in life, so the goal is to make the most out of it by maximizing my own personal growth potential, creating a positive contribution to the community I am a part of, and making my parents proud of the son they have raised. If I can do all three of those things well by the time it's my turn to go, I'd say that's a heck of a life lived.

How's that for what Parkinson's has taught me?

Again, everyone's interpretation of the meaning of life will be different, but hopefully they are similar to mine. There is no such thing as a unique, personal misfortune. Regardless of any problem you can name, chances are millions of others have experienced it in the past, currently have it, or are going to have it in the future.

This will include many people you know as well.

That doesn't minimize the suffering or mean that you aren't a victim of unfortunate circumstances. However, it demonstrates that you are not special and the world isn't conspiring against you, so stop feeling sorry for yourself. We all experience pain. It's inevitable.

What we choose to do with it is up to us.

That is the ultimate meaning of life.

Take a few minutes to ponder your own story and what you interpret the meaning of life to be. Are your daily actions working towards maximizing your own life based on that definition?

Chapter 13: How to Help Someone With Parkinson's Disease

After learning about the seven concepts that I have experienced through my father and Parkinson's disease, hopefully you are able to relate to many of them in your own personal journeys. They have made all the difference in helping me cope with the circumstances and make the best of it, so that the pain and suffering is not for nothing.

I wanted to spend this chapter describing some of the ways in which you can specifically help someone with Parkinson's. Given it's currently the fastest growing neurological disorder in the world[1], I can guarantee you will come across an individual affected by PD sooner rather than later. Some of the concepts and strategies below can also be applied to almost any other disease or circumstance.

Again, there are many commonalities amongst all diseases and illnesses, including caregiving.

How to Help Someone Affected by Parkinson's Disease:

Companionship

One of the most common outcomes of both illness/disease and old age is isolation. As you get older, you inevitably start to lose touch with people you were once close with, stop going to as many social events, your family starts to branch off to create the future generations of the family tree, and people you know will pass away. As sad as this sounds, it is a fact of life. Isolation is especially evident earlier on in the process when illness/disease has affected an individual's ability to work, such as my father's situation.

As much as most of us complain about having to go to work at a full-time job, we often find a lot of value and meaning in the work that we do. It provides an avenue to fill up our time, a chance to participate in social engagement with coworkers, adds structure and routine, and gives us a purpose in life. In fact, a lot of us would be lost both mentally and financially without a job. Sure, a vacation once in a while is much needed, but sitting at home everyday would quickly become boring.

Having written this book during the Coronavirus (Covid-19) quarantine, I'd say almost everyone can now relate to that statement, including myself. Imagine if that was your life for the indefinite future not being able to leave your home with no end in sight. The toll it would have on your mental and physical health would be borderline disastrous. I can't even imagine what my dad has gone through in the 5+ years he's been unemployed. Everyday, he sits at home by himself while my mother goes to work from 9-5.

Add it to the long list of Parkinson's-related consequences that breaks my heart.

Given the prospects of full-time employment isn't a possibility for the majority of those affected by Parkinson's, how can we help in decreasing the feelings of isolation considering the lack of financial resources and limited mobility? After all, a significant portion of those affected by Parkinson's are also unable to drive as well.

My suggestion is the cliché advice to "spend more time with them". The definition of this has changed undoubtedly in the past decade with the advancement of technology and the resources it has created. Spending more time with someone no longer means having to physically be there, although that is still by far the most preferred method. However, there are a multitude of other methods to help make someone feel less lonely and isolated including but not limited to the following:

- Text message
- Video call
- Social media messaging/tagging
- Games online or through cell phone apps
- Email/mail
- Internet message boards/blogs

A lot of these methods don't require much time or effort, but let someone know that you are thinking about them. There is literally no excuse not to be in touch constantly with loved ones anymore!

One of the most effective methods to help cope with isolation/loneliness, and doesn't involve you having to regularly engage, is internet message boards/blogs. These tend to bring together people who have commonalities or similar interests, and often act as support groups to share information and resources. For example, if you look on Facebook, there are a number of groups for those affected by Parkinson's. I happen to have joined some of them and it has been another awesome tool to help me cope and learn.

In the groups, many individuals from all over the world share their own personal stories (after all, every case of Parkinson's is unique with differing degrees of symptoms) and resources including diet, exercise plans, hobbies, and tips/tricks to ease some of the challenges the disease brings. Others will comment, provide suggestions, and show their support.

These internet groups play a vital role in providing support with the knowledge that there are others out there who are going through the same thing and that you are not alone. After all, no matter how much my mother and I are willing to talk about PD, we will never be able to relate to my father or answer some of his questions as well as someone else who also has the disease. In addition, these groups help to play doctor at times when you need an answer ASAP and an appointment isn't possible.

Of course, take any medical advice you read online with caution!

I highly recommend helping your loved ones find these groups if you have not considered them before. A couple platforms I would highly recommend are Facebook, Twitter, and Reddit. They are free to join and make a significant difference in the quality of life for a person with a disease/illness.

Patience

Patience is a virtue that I have found to be extremely helpful over the years in caring for my father, and more so in the recent past as his condition has slowly deteriorated.

Those affected by Parkinson's often have difficulty walking, talking, and performing regular tasks. In most cases, it's not that they can't do it, it's just that it will take longer than usual. Doing these tasks for them and helping minimize the need for movement may seem like a kind gesture - however, they often speed up the symptoms of Parkinson's and help make an individual feel more helpless than they would otherwise. Much like going to the gym, we lose strength in muscles that we don't regularly exercise.

My suggestion is to allow them to continue to perform as many of their routine tasks as possible. Be patient, understand that everything will take longer for an individual affected by Parkinson's, and resist the urge to do it for them. Plan ahead and never be in a hurry, which proves to be a difficult concept to master in a world where speed and convenience are more and more sought after. Allowing someone affected by Parkinson's to continue to complete their daily tasks is both satisfying and provides a sense of achievement or normalcy.

Some examples of scenarios in which your intention to help may actually be detrimental include:

- **Pulling up to the entrance of a storefront to let the individual with Parkinson's out first so that they don't have to walk too far:** This may seem like a nice gesture, but exercise is one of the most important things that slow down the progression of the disease. Given there are already limited opportunities for those with Parkinson's to move, it is important that they utilize every chance they get. Let them walk the extra 50 meters, strengthen their leg muscles, and work on mobility/balance!

- **Communicating on behalf of an individual with Parkinson's in public:** Sometimes, it can be hard to resist the urge to do this in an effort to save time and potential embarrassment. However, people with Parkinson's need to consistently use their voice and lungs to delay the disease inevitably taking a hold of them both. This is especially the case if they experience frequent isolation at home and don't have a job in which communication is necessary. There are many speech and breathing exercises available online as well, and these are strongly recommended for those affected. Also, the inability to communicate for yourself can lead to significant declines in confidence and self-esteem. That is not to say you shouldn't help them if they are clearly struggling, but give them a chance to do it themselves first!

It is important for us to practice patience towards those affected by illness/disease, and understand that sometimes our willingness to help is not actually in the best interest of the individual in the long-run.

Do Your Homework

It is often difficult to relate to an individual with an illness or disease. After all, how can you truly understand what it feels like if you don't have it yourself?

My advice is to educate yourself on the condition in question (in my case Parkinson's Disease) and find out things that may help associated with diet, exercise, natural remedies, etc. Suggest these ideas to the individual affected. Even if they don't choose to utilize the information immediately, at least they now have a better understanding of the disease and options available to make optimal decisions in the future.

Doing so can be frightening, overwhelming, and you might feel distress at the reality of what your loved one is facing. As I stated earlier in the book, I've often struggled with this myself, fearing that I will realize through my research that my father is suffering a lot more than he leads on. In addition, I'm scared that I will read more into the potential causes of the disease, and find that someday there's a high possibility I will also be affected by Parkinson's. Ignorance is bliss. However, the truth is that reality is what it is - the symptoms don't go away or decrease just because you don't read about them.

The likelihood of me being diagnosed with Parkinson's someday in the future doesn't go away because I don't Google it. It's our duty as caregivers and supporters to do our due diligence and come up with ideas to help. Throughout evolution, it has always been beneficial for survival to advance one's knowledge and skill set as much as possible. There's a reason why we continue to learn and grow as we age through life. Imagine how tough it would be to survive if we had the intellect and abilities of a toddler our whole lives.

One of the most successful ways to increase happiness for those living with an illness is to gain as much knowledge about their condition, its nature, treatment, and potential management options. After all, it is our best chance to minimize the symptoms over the long run and lead as normal of a lifestyle as possible. Not to do so because of fear would be unacceptably selfish and cowardly. In fact, it's the most surefire way to allow the illness or disease to win.

Ignorance is not bliss. Ignorance is ignorance.

We're all better than that.

Mental Stimulation

Much along the lines of isolation stated above is the need for consistent mental stimulation. Using our brains has proven to be extremely healthy, as it increases the flow of blood, oxygen, and nutrients, which helps to decrease the likelihood of developing diseases like dementia. It has also been proven to help in areas such as depression, mental health, cognitive abilities, and memory. In addition, solving challenging problems using mental fortitude is very rewarding and help us feel joy and accomplishment.

Most of us get an ample quality of mental stimulation through our jobs, social interactions, educational pursuits, physical exercise, and just general daily issues that occur throughout the course of life. However, for those who are limited by illness/disease/disability, this is hard to come by. Imagine sitting at home, unable able to work, struggle with mobility, limited in financial resources, and not very good with technology, combined with having a significant portion of tasks already done for you by loved ones who are simply trying to help. There aren't many opportunities to keep your brain sharp and be challenged mentally.

This is the issue I have with my father.

He has created pleasure and mental stimulation by playing games on his iPad, and has even found a way to play the Chinese game known as mahjong. For those of you who are unfamiliar with mahjong, the most basic way I can put it is that it is some crazy form of bridge and dominos combined. I must say it's one of the hardest games to learn how to play and master. This has unquestionably helped in keeping my dad's brain engaged, but you can only play it for so many hours in a day before you get bored, especially if you are just playing against the computer. Figuring out a way to pass time alone at home given the circumstances can be a problematic task, especially when there is an endless supply of free time needing to be filled.

In addition to playing mahjong and other games online, my father also spends a sizable portion of his day watching TV. While this isn't necessarily the best form of mental stimulation, it's difficult to find an alternative that will provide endless amounts of entertainment to keep my dad occupied for hours at a time. For my part, I have attempted a number of different things to bring him joy and mental stimulation in those moments of isolation on weekdays while my mother is working her 9-5 job.

They include the following:

- Gifting an iPad to my dad for Christmas
- Books
- Exercise programs
- Riddles (i.e. sudokus and wordsearches)

I've found that while these have proven to work with regards to mental stimulation, over the long-run, everything runs its course and becomes less stimulating until it eventually fades into boredom. That's an inevitable problem that almost all of us experience. In its simplest form, children are obsessed with certain toys and video games, until one day they are bored of them and then it's on to the next shiny new thing. It just becomes more and more difficult to find the next thing given the unique criteria it would have to fit for my dad to be able to get full use out of it.

Currently, the "it" thing is sending emails with questions about his life and past memories. I came across the idea while searching on the internet platform Reddit to see if anyone else had ideas to help solve this problem of mental stimulation. As I said, social media and online communities are fantastic for resources! It led me to a website called StoryWorth.com, which sends one email per week with a question for the individual to answer, and gathers all of the responses at the end of the year into a hardcover book for keepsake and future generations.

The questions range from "describe your wedding day" to "what was your favorite Christmas present?" to "did you have nicknames as a child?". I thought the idea was absolutely brilliant and I hope the creator of Story Worth, Nick Baum, becomes a billionaire someday! I hope he doesn't mind that I am plugging his product.

It has brought so much value and joy into our family, and is something I see as sustainable for months and years to come. There is an endless amount of questions that can be asked (there's even an option in which my father can even choose to write his own!), and it helps to take my dad back to much happier days, mostly before he was diagnosed with Parkinson's.

It's also helped me get to know my parents better, and hear stories they would otherwise have most likely taken to their graves.

I've learned everything from my parents' favorite Christmas memory to the reason they named me

Michael to the most difficult decision they've ever had to make. I strongly recommend it for everyone to try.

Each week, my father's submission is usually almost double the length of my mother's. This tells me that it's mentally stimulating and he's finding tremendous joy in doing it, despite my mother's gripes about having to proofread or translate his submissions as a result of his poor English. It also helps to occupy his time throughout the week, since the questions require personal reflection and details of our memories often come back in pieces the more we think about them.

A particular answer that sticks out to me since we started doing this exercise about half a year ago is from week 19. The question was "Describe your marriage". The answer my father input was short but perhaps the most meaningful response I've received so far through this (pardon the grammar but I wanted to copy it word for word):

"We have been married since year 1987, it is more than 30 years. It is not easy to maintain a relationship for such a long time. We are all human beings and we have good and bad moments always. For me, even though I am a Parkinson patient, I would still say that I am the luckiest man in this world. I have a very beautiful, wise and nice lady as my wife and I also have a very good, clever and filial piety son. Also he will bring us a very nice lady as our daughter-in-law."

My father summarized our whole family story and all seven concepts in less than 100 words. My heart couldn't be more full after reading that response.

Really helps you put things into perspective, doesn't it?

Our conversations afterwards about their submissions are memories I will cherish for the rest of my life. It's mental stimulation, family bonding, and legacy, all wrapped into one simple idea. You can even execute it yourself. Come up with a list of questions and send them on a weekly basis by email to your parents, or sign up for a membership with StoryWorth. I guarantee reading their responses will be the best part of your week!

At the end of the day, I still have trouble in finding ways to help my father and improve his quality of life. How do you help someone with a disease that forces you to struggle with the most miniscule daily tasks and has no cure? How do you look someone in the eye and tell them that everything will be okay when you both know that it's probably not going to be?

I ponder this on a daily basis, and will spend the rest of my life trying to figure it out. After all, you can blame yourself for just about anything if you think about it long enough. If we didn't move to Canada, a move they made for the best interests of my future, would my dad still end up getting Parkinson's? Could it have been some toxin or pesticide he was exposed to here that he wouldn't have encountered in Hong Kong?

Basketball is one of the biggest ways that my father and I bond. We both grew up playing, and we both coached. My parents actually first met on a basketball court in Hong Kong, and my dad was actually my mom's coach at one point... while they were dating! It's literally in my blood.

Therefore, it's only fitting that one of my favorite concepts is from the book of a famous individual in the basketball world, who struggled through his own personal battles before ultimately succumbing to cancer in 2016.

"Hope is not a strategy." - Craig Sager[15]

I take this concept to heart, and understand that simply wishing for things to magically get better isn't exactly a winning strategy. As a result, the best way I have found to help someone with an incurable disease is to raise funds and awareness in their honor, so that a cure can eventually be found.

Fight the root cause of the issue, and not the subsequent results. It may end up being too late to save my father, but hopefully no one in the future will ever have to suffer from this horrible disease.

We are all in this together.

Nobody fights alone. #BeatParky

Below are a couple of organizations I would recommend checking out if you are looking to donate towards Parkinson's:

Michael J Fox Foundation (www.michaeljfox.org)

Rock Steady Boxing (https://www.rocksteadyboxing.org/) - if there is a local chapter near where you reside, I would suggest donating directly to them!

American Parkinson Disease Association (https://www.apdaparkinson.org/)

Parkinson Canada (https://www.parkinson.ca/)

Chapter 14: What's Next?

What's next?

This is a question I constantly ponder, and one of the numerous questions I have that cannot be answered at the moment. I often play out inevitable scenarios in my head when I sit alone with my thoughts. The future for my family is both scary and depressing, and I'm often reminded that currently science tells us things will literally only get worse.

One of the things I often ponder is my own future. As mentioned in the chapter entitled "What is Parkinson's disease?" near the beginning of the book, all of the literature/research indicates that there seems to be a multitude of different ways an individual can get Parkinson's, and it includes some combination of surroundings and genetics unique to each case.

Obviously, I can't help but wonder if I will one day end up being diagnosed with Parkinson's as well.

I'm encouraged by the fact that my father was the first person in our extended family to have PD, but then again science and technology are a lot better these days, and it is easier to identify the symptoms and properly diagnose them.

In addition, the past is not always an indication of the future; it can sometimes be a little haunting to look at my father and think that I could very well be looking into my own future.

I certainly hope that science and medicine will have progressed significantly by then to find more effective forms of treatment to minimize/halt symptoms. A cure would also be great! There are certain mass marketed DNA tests that help to determine whether individuals have potential genetic mutations, which I could take to determine if I am more susceptible to developing Parkinson's in the future, but I'm not sure if I would even want to know. I spent the last chapter explaining that ignorance isn't bliss, but in this scenario where nothing can be done if a genetic mutation was found, it might be.

All I can do is to make a concentrated effort to decrease my exposure to harmful pesticides, toxins, and solvents, eat healthier, drink more coffee, and exercise more. The rest is up to luck, and if you've taken anything away from the chapter on luck, you know you've got to put yourself in the right situation to give yourself a chance. I believe continuing with these actions will provide me with the best opportunity to be "lucky" enough to avoid Parkinson's.

I worry about the mental health of my parents. A significant portion of people with Parkinson's also develop Alzeheimer's, which would present another countless number of problems for both of my parents. In addition, there has been ample research indicating that people with Parkinson's who have undergone DBS (deep brain stimulation) surgery go through significant personality changes, which drastically affect their thinking and decision-making. I can already see the changes that my father has gone through since DBS surgery about five years ago.

I also worry about my mother's mental state; she has been an absolute rock throughout these past 15+ years and has never shown even a slight crack. For everything that she has been through, I wish I could give her the world.

Then again, she is only human and everyone has a breaking point.

I think about the amount of times that my parents have cried as a result of Parkinson's. Given the amount of times that I have throughout the years, I'd be naive to think they hadn't cried as much also. One of the most painful things in this process is knowing that there isn't much I can do to take that pain away from them.

Something else I constantly think about is the inevitable passing of my parents. One would assume that it would just be thoughts about my father, but they're often split 50-50 between both of my parents. What would happen if my mother was to pass away before my father? It would create a significant burden on me both mentally and financially, having to take care of my father. As I get older and have more responsibilities/ambitions arise surrounding my career, family, goals, and dreams, it becomes a greater and greater sacrifice if the scenario were to ever occur.

It is a bit of a Catch-22. My parents sacrificed everything for me to live the life I currently do with the freedom to dream without a ceiling, yet taking care of my father would undoubtedly become priority number one and would take up the majority of my time and resources.

On to my father. It's funny - I spent my whole life as a child thinking my parents were invincible. There wasn't a problem or need I had that was too big for my parents to fix or provide, and in a sense, I still feel that way today.

However, at the same time, I often ponder about the continual progression of PD in my father. I live with the reality that there is a decent chance my father may not be with us anymore even three years from now, and might not get to see his future grandchildren. Even if he is, he probably won't be physically capable of holding the baby or playing with him/her. That breaks my heart to even think about. It motivates me to maximize the time we still have left together, and do everything I possibly can to make his remaining years on earth as happy as possible.

To bring it full circle, that's why I wrote this book. I'm not here to preach about how everything is sunshine and rainbows; this shit is real life. It's heart-breaking, family-separating, depression-inducing, and downright unfair, but we must find a way to make the most of it.

After all, what choice do we really have?

I hope this book helped you understand that we all experience difficulties and that our stories aren't actually all that different. You don't have to be famous or even successful to tell your story and have an impact. But most of all, I hope you now realize that if you look beneath the surface, you'll find there is a lot of good that can come out of unfortunate situations.

There's no denying the costs and pains of illness and disease, but make it a goal to force yourself to find some benefits in the suffering. It will improve the life and happiness of everyone affected.

I'll leave you with this.

During the beginning phase of my interest in entrepreneurship, I came across a podcast called "StartUp Podcast" by Gimlet Media. It's details the journey of entrepreneurs trying to get their ideas off the ground and build legitimate, successful business.

In season one, the host Alex Blumberg attempts to pitch billionaire investor Chris Sacca on his idea of starting a podcast network business. As the pitch progresses, Chris asks Alex a question that changed my whole perspective on my family's journey:

"What is your unfair advantage?" [22]

In other words, Chris wanted to know what Alex does better than everyone else that differentiates him and makes Gimlet Media worth investing in? There are thousands of other podcasts out there, all believing they'll be successful when they first start. What gives Alex an advantage over them that is hard to replicate?

I've thought about how this relates to my own personal life and entrepreneurial pursuits. What makes me so special and different than anyone else?

I didn't graduate at the top of my class. I'm not an expert in anything. I've never won anything significant in my life. I wasn't the valedictorian. I don't do one thing better than anyone I know. I'm 6'0", 180 pounds, and the definition of an average human being.

I spent months trying to figure out what my unfair advantage could possibly be.

And then it all came together.

My development of the aforementioned seven concepts through my family's experience with Parkinson's disease has provided me with a perspective on life that really can't be replicated, unless you've been through a similar journey involving illness/disease.

So, tell your story, volunteer, face your fears, help a friend in need, check off your bucket list, pay it forward, travel the world, break down barriers, donate, chase your dreams, build something meaningful, and live life to the fullest.

Because someone you love dearly suffered a pain/misfortune so unreasonably unfair - it would be a shame to let it all go to waste.

I know I won't... I've already lost too much.

#BeatParky

References:

1. Dorsey, R., Sherer, T., Okun, M. S., & Bloem, B. R. (2020). Ending Parkinson's Disease: A Prescription For Action. New York: PublicAffairs.

2. Statistics. (n.d.). Retrieved April 19, 2020, from https://www.parkinson.org/Understanding-Parkinsons/Statistics

3. Young-Onset Parkinson's Disease. (n.d.). Retrieved April 19, 2020, from https://www.michaeljfox.org/news/young-onset-parkinsons-disease

4. Passion. (n.d.). Retrieved April 19, 2020, from https://www.merriam-webster.com/dictionary/passion

5. Ballard, C. (2018, May 2). Same Warrior, New Battle: Brian Grant's fight with Parkinson's. Retrieved from https://www.si.com/nba/2018/05/02/brian-grant-parkinsons-disease-trail-blazers-heat-michael-j-fox-pat-riley

6. Empathy. (n.d.). Retrieved April 19, 2020, from https://www.merriam-webster.com/dictionary/empathy

7. Luck. (n.d.). Retrieved April 19, 2020, from https://www.merriam-webster.com/dictionary/luck

8. Altucher, J. (2016, October 20). Chuck Klosterman – but what if we're wrong? Retrieved from https://yourstory.com/2016/10/chuck-klosterman

9. Regret. (n.d.). Retrieved April 19, 2020, from https://www.merriam-webster.com/dictionary/regret

10. Toughness. (n.d.). Retrieved April 19, 2020, from https://www.merriam-webster.com/dictionary/toughness

11. Sadness. (n.d.). Retrieved April 19, 2020, from https://www.merriam-webster.com/dictionary/sadness

12. Mark Manson. (2020, February 28). The Feedback Loop from Hell. Retrieved from https://markmanson.net/feedback-loop-from-

hell

13. Text of the 2014 Commencement address by Bill and Melinda Gates. (2014, June 15). Retrieved from https://news.stanford.edu/news/2014/june/gates-commencement-remarks-061514.html

14. Love. (n.d.). Retrieved April 19, 2020, from https://www.merriam-webster.com/dictionary/love

15. Sager, C. (2016). Living Out Loud: Sports, Cancer, And The Things Worth Fighting For. New York, NY: Flatiron Books.

16. Manson, M. (2019). Everything Is F*cked: A Book About Hope. New York, NY: Harper, an Imprint of HarperCollinsPublishers.

17. A quote by Anonymous. (n.d.). Retrieved April 19, 2020, from https://www.goodreads.com/quotes/6395093-someone-once-told-me-the-definition-of-hell-on-your

18. Monty Python. (2015, December 22). Monty Python - Always Look On The Bright Side Of Life (Official Lyric Video) [Video]. Youtube.

https://www.youtube.com/watch?v=X_-q9xeOgG4

19. 12 Famous Quotes to Inspire the Volunteer in All of Us. (2017, April 26). Retrieved April 19, 2020, from https://ca.finance.yahoo.com/news/12-famous-quotes-inspire-volunteer-155638253.html

20. Groth, A. (2012, July 24). You're The Average Of The Five People You Spend The Most Time With. Retrieved April 19, 2020, from https://www.businessinsider.com/jim-rohn-youre-the-average-of-the-five-people-you-spend-the-most-time-with-2012-7

21. Amanda Marshall. (2010, September 27). Amanda Marshall - Everybody's Got A Story (Official Video) [Video]. Youtube. https://www.youtube.com/watch?v=3kZ-gG4r0zI&feature=emb_logo

22. Gimlet. (2014, April 5). StartUp Podcast: Gimlet 1: How Not to Pitch a Billionaire on Apple Podcasts. Retrieved April 19, 2020, from https://podcasts.apple.com/us/podcast/gimlet-1-how-not-to-pitch-a-billionaire/id913805339?i=1000318522342

Thank you for reading!

#BeatParky

Manufactured by Amazon.ca
Bolton, ON

13125123R00118